Michael Bruce

Michael Bruce is a composer and lyricist who has written scores and songs for many theatre productions around the UK, in London and New York. After training at the Liverpool Institute for Performing Arts (LIPA) he worked as a musical director and musician. In 2007 he won the Notes for the Stage prize for songwriting run by the *Stage* newspaper, which led to a concert of his musical-theatre work being staged at the Apollo Theatre on Shaftesbury Avenue. Following the success of this, his album *Unwritten Songs* was released and debuted at number one on the iTunes vocal chart.

He has held the position of Composer-in-Residence at both the Bush Theatre and the Donmar Warehouse in London. His work at the Donmar has included scores for *The Vote, Privacy, Coriolanus, Trelawny of the Wells, Berenice, Philadelphia, Here I Come!, The Physicists* and *The Recruiting Officer*; at the National Theatre: *Sunset at the Villa Thalia, The Beaux Stratagem, Man and Superman, Strange Interlude* and *Men Should Weep*; and at the Royal Shakespeare Company: *The Two Gentlemen of Verona* and *Candide*. He has written scores for shows at the Old Vic, Hampstead Theatre, the Finborough Theatre and the Lyric Hammersmith, and in the West End his credits include *Much Ado About Nothing, Relatively Speaking, Hay Fever* and *Noises Off*. On Broadway his work has included *Les Liaisons Dangereuses* and *The Winslow Boy*.

Michael has worked extensively as an arranger, orchestrator and conductor – and is also incredibly proud to have played table tennis for Scotland in his youth.

Michael Bruce

Writing Music *for the* Stage

A Practical Guide for Theatremakers

Michael Bruce

Foreword by Josie Rourke

NICK HERN BOOKS
London
www.nickhernbooks.co.uk

A Nick Hern Book

Writing Music for the Stage
first published in Great Britain in 2016
as a paperback original by Nick Hern Books Limited,
The Glasshouse, 49a Goldhawk Road, London W12 8QP

Designed and typeset by Nick Hern Books, London
Printed and bound in Great Britain by
Ashford Colour Press, Gosport, Hampshire

A CIP catalogue record for this book
is available from the British Library

ISBN 978 1 84842 393 0

Contents

Foreword

Josie Rourke
Artistic Director, Donmar Warehouse

I'm writing this in a rehearsal room in New York. We're downtown at The Public Theater, working on the American premiere of James Graham's play, *Privacy*. We've spent the afternoon working with Michael Bruce on a new scene that James has just written. It's essentially two scenes, two locations overlapping. I think that it needs underscoring to bind it into a single movement, and I asked Michael – overnight – to pull together some music for it.

I'm moving in between the actors and Michael: directing the new scene, asking Michael to change and rewrite the music as I go. He is calm, curious, pragmatic, and breathtakingly fast. Really, the actors should be focused on their new lines, and new tracks. But as Michael works away in the room, taking notes, manipulating the musical sketches he's written to fit and express what's happening in front of him, I can see the actors begin to slow, observe and – finally – just stop and stare at him. They're right to. It is a wonder.

Sometimes in the British theatre, we prize speed over all other qualities. But allow me – for half a heartbeat – to dwell shamelessly in that questionable value system, as I tell you that no one I have ever worked with can match the creative pace of Michael Bruce. It was a joy – but not a surprise – when I learned that he was a junior table tennis champion. And it's not that he's prolific. He's instantaneous.

Several years ago, when I was Artistic Director of The Bush Theatre, our Arts Council Officer and I had a conversation about musical theatre. I said that it was a shame that new composers didn't get to spend enough time around new playwrights. A few weeks later (it was near year end) he produced a small sum of money – and Michael Bruce.

Michael was in residence for a year at The Bush – composing music for new plays. In the midst of that, I freelanced, directing quite a big show at the National Theatre. The play – *Men Should Weep* – was set over three floors of a Glaswegian tenement, a sort of *Rear Window* concept, with insanely complicated scene changes. At the very last moment, the (quite fancy, not theatre) composer we had asked to write music for the play, slid quietly off the map. We had a huge 'transitions rehearsal' planned and needed someone to replace him yesterday. I hadn't been able to persuade them to let me hire Michael the first time around but, cometh the hour... He was at the rehearsal room in two hours flat. He saw our final runthrough the next day, and wrote and recorded the most wonderful score in three days.

His ability is cultivated from a place of true collaboration. He doesn't just look at his part, he feels out the whole. Often, during previews, his notes are the most valuable. 'I don't think people really get what this is meant to be...', 'Right, what is that bit meant to be doing?' Like all great composers he can lift you into lyricism, but like all great collaborators, he can also pop your pretension. There is no one who has – more reliably – told the emperor that he appears to be naked than Michael Bruce.

From his gorgeous score for *Les Liaisons Dangereuses*, to the beautiful folk music he wrote for *The Recruiting Officer*; from his harsh, propulsive music for *Coriolanus*, to his 1980s tribute pop for *Much Ado About Nothing*, Michael can pretty much write anything. I don't think that comes from a place of pastiche or want of the original. I think it comes from collaboration and respect. He really cares about what the work means, and has no pride, no preciousness about throwing everything away to start again. And – like his instincts – Michael's music is wonderful: inclusive, original, respectful and in its rightness – sheer joy.

June 2016

Tuning Up: Preface

The truth is, I never set out to write music for the theatre. As with so many things in life, I just sort of fell into it when I wasn't paying attention. It turns out to have been one of the best accidents I've ever had.

Before my first experience of composing music for a play, I had toured the world as a musical director on cruise ships and had some success with small-scale musical theatre and albums (including a brief stint at number one on the brilliantly vague 'vocal chart' on iTunes) – so I wasn't completely green. But in terms of the world of plays or 'straight theatre', as some people alarmingly call it, I was entering the professional arena pretty fresh. I've tried to set out in this book the things I've learned about the creative process, and the necessary skills one needs to survive in the world of theatre composition. Hopefully you will find some of what's in the following pages useful, relevant, or at least diverting.

The knowledge and skill required to write decent (I won't say great) scores for plays forces a composer to examine his craft, follow a brief and work quickly, and be able to write music that supports and enhances drama. A lot of incredibly successful composers (perhaps most of them) have, at some point in their careers, written music for the stage. As it turns out, the world seems not to have noticed. That's another part of the reason for this book: an attempt to treat the process and the endeavour with the appropriate credit it deserves.

What follows is by no means intended as a definitive rulebook for writing music for the theatre. There are plenty of books out there detailing the important issues of, for example, counterpoint and harmony. Instead, this is my attempt to apply a general musical knowledge to the theatre and the art of storytelling through music and drama. It represents my current thoughts on the subject and the methods I have used to approach my profession.

Writing music for the theatre presents the opportunity to exercise versatility as a composer. Each play will present new challenges, as will every director, company and venue. The best education you can get is by doing, learning on the job, and tackling a production, whether it's at the National Theatre or in a school hall. This book tries to lend a hand and explain how the process in the professional theatre works, but hopefully it will be applicable to any context you might find yourself in. Likewise, whilst it's aimed mainly at theatre composers, I hope if you're a director, a writer, an actor, a designer, a producer, or involved in theatre at any level, it will help you to understand how music can work – and how ideas in a composer's head end up being heard by an audience, helping to create an imaginary world and tell a story on stage.

A Note on Gender

Throughout I've used 'he' or 'his' to denote both genders. This doesn't reflect anything except a reluctance to construct convoluted sentences.

▶ *A Note on Case Studies*

Many of the case studies in this book, appearing in grey panels, are accompanied by online excerpts of my scores. Where the play symbol appears, visit the following Soundcloud playlist to listen to the clip:

soundcloud.com/nickhernbooks/sets/writingmusicforthestage

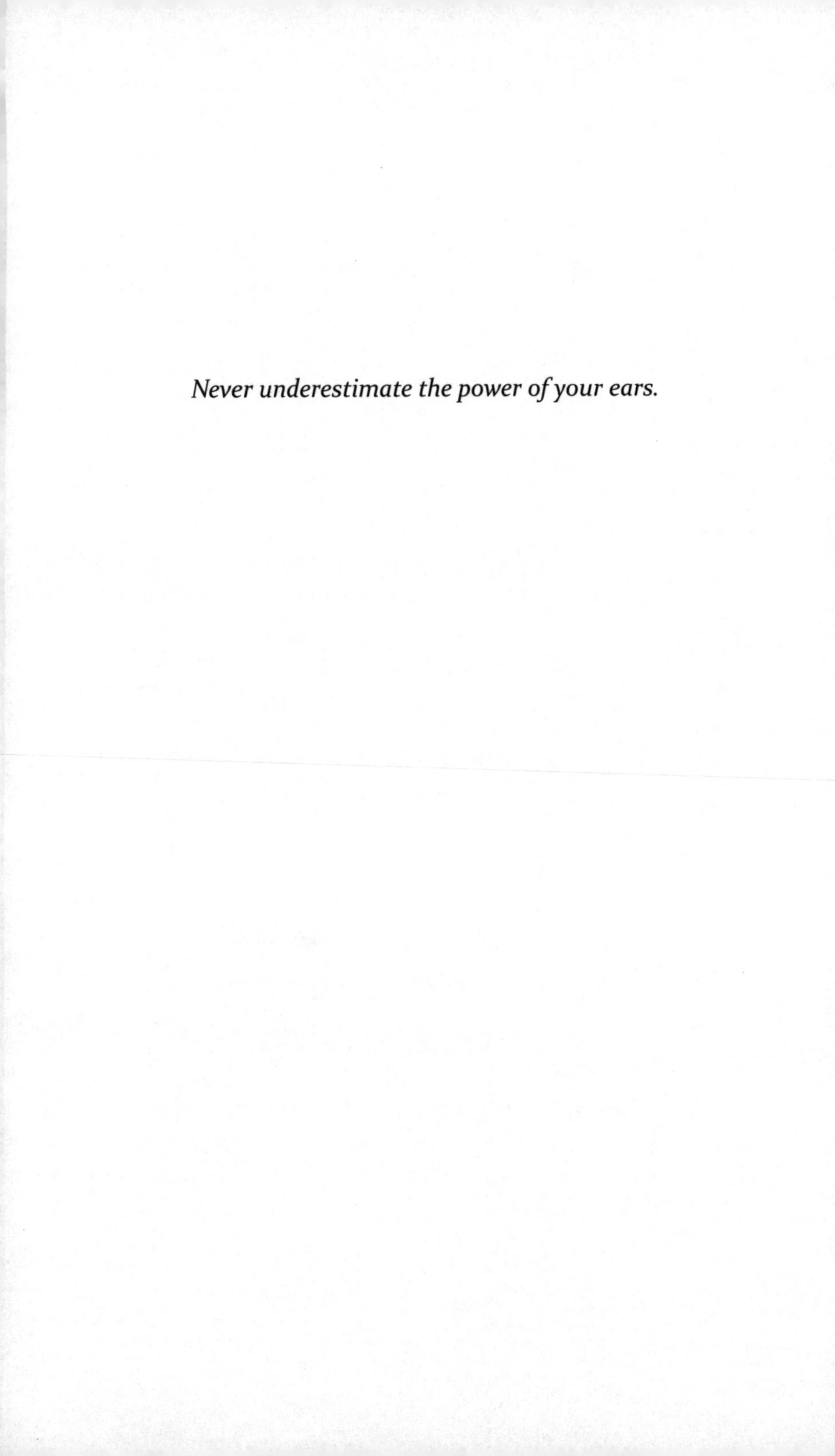

Never underestimate the power of your ears.

Overture:
Introduction

'I want to do something creative,
not just easy.'
Johann Sebastian Bach

Our Beginnings with Music

Listening to music is an experience expressly connected with emotion. From the main stage at Glastonbury to street carnivals in Rio de Janeiro to the high-school choir singing a medley from *Mamma Mia!*, the human capacity to connect with and be affected by an organised combination of tones and vibrations is a phenomenon that follows us from the womb.

Professor of Musicology Richard Parncutt asks, 'Why should music be so emotional when, unlike other behaviours and experiences such as love, pain and hunger, it is not critical for human survival?' The theory he puts forward is that during prenatal development, infants learn to associate audible sound and movement patterns with the mother's changing physical and hormonal state, and that this may be one of our primary early interactions with music. Perhaps when similar patterns of sound and movement are recreated at later points in life the corresponding emotional response may stem from this infant experience.[1]

Of course, this doesn't really detail why certain pieces of music are more effective than others at stimulating certain emotions, but part of the magic of music is its mysterious power over us. Some think that rather like a conjuring trick, it loses its power when it is interrogated and explained in scientific terms. I would argue, however, that even after analysis, music still holds our emotions to ransom, and particularly interestingly when played in a dramatic context such as in the theatre or cinema.

There are many articles and intellectual treatises on the sometimes 'scientific' reasoning behind why it might be that certain pieces of music make us feel a certain way, but approaching it from an academic viewpoint and applying abstract musical terminology tends to get us nowhere closer to the beautifully secluded heart of the matter.

This is not to say that musical critique does not have its place, but I don't think it's all that inspiring for the burgeoning artist who wants to expand his horizons and understand the compositional process. What I think we can say is: all music is written within a framework, and that framework varies depending on many social, historical and aspirational factors. The mine of musical interpretation and commentary is deep, but we don't learn as much from literature as we do from the composers themselves. Each new piece of music is informed by and descended from some expression that came before, no matter how tangibly. Even if a composer heads out on a new road that seems previously completely untravelled, his compositional choices will still be influenced by those roads he eschews. If we think of the vibrations and tones given to us by the laws of physics as akin to a box of paints, then our musical heritage is as colourful and expressive as that of all the great masters in any National Gallery.

But unlike painting or sculpture, music is not frozen in time. In Leonard Bernstein's 1955 telecast on *The Art of Conducting*, he said: 'Music... exists in the medium of time. It is time itself that must be carved up, moulded and remoulded until it becomes, like a statue, a fixed form and shape.' Music can therefore never be perceived in a snapshot. Music never stands still; the canvas on which composers paint is actually time itself.

Live theatre is like live music, in that it's only alive when it's moving. Every moment is fleeting and never to be repeated in the exact same way again. Of course, like music, it *can* be repeated (and needs to be, usually eight times a week, if it's to be successful), but the contextual factors of a particular performance, with a particular audience, on a particular day, and with a particular cast and crew, dictate that no two performances can ever be identical. Theatre, like music, is in the business of telling stories and in the examination and reflection of the human condition, but because music is so ephemeral its critical interpretation is often a little abstract. It can instantly set a tone or mood, create momentum, encourage contemplation or affect emotional depth; it can lift the heart to the stars or drag the soul through the gutter, but when combined with the literal exposition of stories in a theatrical setting, music can lift a prosaic moment into something quite extraordinary.

A Brief History of Music in Theatre

Theatre is not confined to the West End of London or the twinkling lights of Broadway; theatre is everywhere. It's on the news and in the local pub. It's in the chamber of the House of Commons. Theatre is where drama is. And drama happens where conflict arises. If you wander through the halls of any high school in Middle America or college in the UK you will find an English or Drama department reading (at the very least) and perhaps even staging plays. Plays are conflicts dramatised. They tell us a lot about ourselves, they cultivate curiosity, stimulate ideas, encourage our minds to be subtle and flexible, jump-start our imaginations and show us new perspectives on our lives.

Theatre has long been linked with music. The use of incidental music in plays may possibly have originated in ancient Greek or Roman theatre, but there is certainly the documented use of songs and music as a link between scenes in the English comedy *Ralph Roister Doister* by Nicholas Udall, written in the mid-sixteenth century. Music was also used as an essential accompaniment to sixteenth- and seventeenth-century festivals and the pageants called masques.[2] Shakespeare's plays are full of songs, dances and calls for incidental music, which is unsurprising, as Elizabethan life seemed to thrive on the joys of music. Publishers in London produced scores of consort pieces, madrigals and broadside ballads, as many of the educated could read and play music; their most favoured instruments being the recorder, lute and viola da gamba.[3]

Through the character of Lorenzo in *The Merchant of Venice*, Shakespeare gave us a fair treatise on the value of music and song:

> The man that hath no music in himself,
> Nor is not moved with concord of sweet sounds,
> Is fit for treasons, stratagems and spoils;
> The motions of his spirit are dull as night
> And his affections dark as Erebus:
> Let no such man be trusted. Mark the music.

Evidence of the prevalence of music in plays in Shakespeare's time can be seen in the theatrical impresario Philip Henslowe's surviving papers, which contain details of the operational requirements of Elizabethan public theatres. They include:

> The Enventary of Clownes Sewtes and Hermetes Sewtes, with dievers other sewtes, as followeth, 1598, the 10 of March... iij [3] trumpettes and a drum, and a trebel viall, a basse vial, a bandore [a bass cittern], a sytteren [cittern: a stringed Renaissance instrument which looks like a modern-day flat-back mandolin].[4]

The Licensing Act of 1737 granted only two 'patent theatres' in London the rights to present dramatic plays, Covent Garden Theatre and Drury Lane. All scripts had to be vetted by the Lord Chamberlain and his Examiners of Plays. Smaller venues could be granted 'burletta' licenses which allowed 'plays with music' to be performed, but never serious drama. This legislation led to the divide in British theatrical performance between what was known as legitimate and illegitimate theatre.[5] Venues in London were often prosecuted or closed when they strayed too far from the remit of their license. In her article 'Theatre in the Nineteenth Century', Jacky Bratton considers that

> the very restrictions that forbade the new theatres to do Shakespeare or other straight plays perhaps partly inspired the brilliant ingenuity and inventiveness of entertainment at this time. Unlicensed premises relied on silent or musically-accompanied action, physical theatre, animals and acrobatics, and thus both

> melodrama and Victorian pantomime were developed...a more spectacular, visual style took over from the static eighteenth-century emphasis on the spoken word.[6]

In 1843 the Patent Act was abolished allowing all theatres to stage dramas. Curiously this didn't lead to many more productions of classic plays, but to a more experimental and innovative variety of entertainment to suit the masses. This precipitated the birth of the West End as we know it today. The two patent theatres became venues for two types of musical theatre – opera at Covent Garden and the annual pantomime at Drury Lane. Emphasis was on the spectacular. 'As Victorian technology – electric lighting and hydraulics – advanced, the scale and excitement of the on-stage battles, storms, explosions and transformations grew, until they slid seamlessly, at the turn of the twentieth century, into the new medium of film.'[7]

Some of our most eminent and long-standing composers wrote a great deal of music for plays. Henry Purcell, the renowned Restoration composer, built a large part of his career on it, and Jean-Baptiste Lully wrote incidental music for the royal comédies-ballets that prefigured the development of the French opera and opéra-comique.[8] In the seventeenth century, Henry Purcell was writing music for English plays and in the 1800s, Edvard Grieg's score for Ibsen's *Peer Gynt* was nearly ninety minutes long. As Anthony Tommasini mentioned in a recent *New York Times* article:

> The original 1876 production lasted some five hours. Grieg later extracted two popular orchestral suites from the score. But those who know 'In the Hall of the Mountain King' only from the suite would be stunned to hear the chilling original version which includes a shrieking chorus and thunderous percussion. Mendelssohn's beloved incidental music for Shakespeare's *Midsummer Night's Dream* is so elaborate that it was not hard for later composers to fashion the various pieces into an evening-length ballet score.[9]

Other notable classical composers who wrote incidental music for plays include Beethoven, Schubert, Handel, Arthur Sullivan and, of course, our old friend Leonard Bernstein.

Music in the Modern Theatre

Over time, scores written for plays have utilised a huge variety of instrument ensembles. From the relatively small Elizabethan consorts in Shakespeare's day to the huge orchestral forces employed by Grieg, trends have constantly shifted and continue to do so. In terms of utilising grand orchestral ensembles in music for the play, 18 February 1933 could be viewed as a watershed moment. Germany, which had since the end of the First World War been a crucible for creativity, art and composition, was to play host for the premiere of Kurt Weill's score for *Der Silbersee* by Georg Kaiser. It premiered simultaneously in Leipzig, Magdeburg and Erfurt, featuring a full orchestra and chorus and has been described as the last 'serious play' to do so. The composer himself insisted on it being called 'a play with music', but it also falls into the categories of 'music drama' or 'singspiel'. An anti-Third Reich play, it was banned by the Nazis after sixteen performances and was the last production these artists worked on before they were forced to flee for their lives. As Charles Hazlewood puts it in his BBC radio series about *Der Silbersee*:

> This is literally the last great jewel of what was an extraordinary period of cultural creativity: the Weimar years of Germany... an age that spawned talents the like of Berthold Brecht, composers like Kurt Weill, Hanns Eisler [and] Paul Dessau... the theatre director Erwin Piscator created the fertile ground out of which grew Dada. [It was] a really amazing time. Nine days after that premiere, on 27 February, the Reichstag burned down, and following it, Hitler's suspension of civil liberties... you get a sense of the piece – it's on a sort of knife edge between the end of one glorious age and the beginning of a much darker one.[10]

In more recent times, generally due to something as boring as budget constraints, the trend for productions of plays is to use smaller instrumental ensembles or recorded music. Of course, musical theatre, opera and ballet all still commonly feature much larger ensembles and choruses, but in terms of what could be considered a 'play' there are very few which still feature a full orchestral accompaniment. There has always been (of course) the option to use pre-existing music for a production (as long as the relevant rights are cleared), but in recent years with the development of technology and the relative affordability of recording equipment, it has become more affordable and practical for original music to be composed and recorded for plays. It's only relatively recently that theatres stopped playing recordings from reels and started using computer software to fire their pre-recorded cues. Of course, not all theatre music is pre-recorded – there are still stage productions of plays that utilise live musicians, but these are, sadly, less common.

The Role of the Composer in Theatre

Theatre composers are creators. They work in a team with other 'creatives' including directors, set, costume, lighting and sound designers, movement directors and choreographers – but fundamentally they must work alone to provide a musical response to, and context for, the words of the playwright. They need to possess a well-grounded knowledge of, and talent for, composition, but they must also be able to work within the specifications of a playwright or director's brief. They must be able to juggle an inquisitive and experimental creativity with the ability to deliver on deadline. Composers in the theatre frequently perform multiple roles as arranger, copyist, lyricist, musical director, producer and fixer. They need to be able to work quickly and under pressure and are not afforded the luxury of big budgets or long time frames. The 'father of film music' Max Steiner, who also wrote music for theatre, put the reality of a jobbing composer into perspective:

> I have written 186 scores for movies in the fourteen years I've been in Hollywood... and most of them were written on less than three weeks' notice. I wrote the three hours and forty-five minutes of original music for *Gone with the Wind* plus the score for another film and supervised

> the recording of both, all within the space of four weeks. I did it by getting exactly fifteen hours of sleep during those four weeks and working steadily the rest of the time. You can't be a Beethoven under those conditions.

There are, of course, many strands to the dramatic medium – ballets, operas, films, musicals – and though we may touch on some of these briefly, there are many books and articles already written about them. This book considers the often overlooked yet vital function of the musical score in a play.

Act One:

Preparation

'In the long run, any words about music are less important than the music.'

Dmitri Shostakovich

Getting Started

First things first, you'll want and need to read the script. This is, of course, providing there is one (which may not always be the case if, for example, you're working on a devised piece), but for the purposes of this chapter let's assume that you have been given a draft of the script at some point before the first day of rehearsals. Try to read it with an open mind before formulating any ideas as to what a play is about or how the music might function or sound. Even if you've seen the play before or you think you know it; if you've seen the movie or read the Wikipedia page, it is still important to begin your process with the text. Try to read it from a neutral standpoint and don't worry too much about the score yet.

Reading a play is a skill in itself. Many intelligent and successful creative people struggle to read plays. Visualising scenes right off the page is a tricky but useful skill to develop. Play texts by their nature leave room for interpretation by actors, directors, designers, etc. Sometimes it takes weeks of rehearsal to make sense of a moment, a line or a stage direction – but making these discoveries is a stimulating and essential part of the process. As a composer you should be interested in these discoveries as they may inform your own work, but they will happen in time. Not knowing how the production will function stylistically, at this stage you should take what you can from what is set down in black and white, even if it's just a preliminary understanding of plot, character and setting.

Eventually it will be your interpretation as an artist, what you bring to and (hopefully) add to the production, that will help to make the music an integral part of the whole, but staging a play is a process that takes input from many people with different areas of expertise. Often you may find the text only really begins to come alive at the first reading with the cast; just hearing different voices speaking the words can shed light on a scene you may have struggled to comprehend fully on your own.

Before this point you'll be looking to get certain things from the script. It's possible you will have a preliminary meeting with the director before the rehearsal period to discuss ideas, so it's always good to go to those meetings with a bit of background knowledge. Do some general research into the play's author and the time and place it was written and set. Take a look at the play's history, clock any previous productions and generally become aware of its original context and place in the canon. Of course, depending on a director's wishes, the production may be taken in a wholly new or unexpected direction, but all background research is worthwhile at this point in the process.

Music Spotting

After you've read the play in its entirety you'll hopefully have a grasp of plot and a general sense of style. You should then turn your attention to music spotting: the process of identifying all the moments in a play where music *might* be used and how. Make a note of where songs are written into the script, and any other music that the playwright has expressly asked for. In addition to this, you should look out for other unscripted places you think it might be appropriate, such as scene changes and where you think underscore might be effective. Don't worry too much about exactly how you'll use underscore at this stage: it will become more obvious after you've spoken to the director and once you're in the rehearsal room.

Music can function many different ways in a play. Many include dances or songs, some of which will be unique to the show. Some may have original lyrics printed in the text or reference existing songs that are already recorded, published or well known. Sometimes it isn't obvious into which camp a song belongs and you'll have to do a bit of digging. It's seldom that a play arrives with sheet music attached, but it does happen occasionally. Particularly with an old play, you may struggle to find out whether a melody was ever recorded or written down. Often these melodies tend to be lost over the years, but you shouldn't let that worry you too much. Of Shakespeare's many plays, only a very few of the original song settings have survived. When you write new music for a play you can compose exactly to the specifications of the production you're working on. Sometimes even if a melody does exist, it may be the better choice to write a new one, unless it's incredibly famous or expressly integral.

Sometimes, however, a director might (quite justly) wish to use sourced music from the original period of the play and you will find yourself arranging rather than composing. He may even want to use contemporary music that's already in the public consciousness. It's important to note that sometimes your job as a composer is not to compose anew but to rearrange or reimagine existing works. Tailored period music can add to the authenticity of a production if it's an appropriate choice. The important thing is not to let your ego get in the way; you can be creative in whatever role you inhabit. Quite often in these instances, you'll find the score ends up being a mixture of both new and pre-existing music – and will be much the better for it.

Regularly with a play, a lot of your time will be spent composing music for scene changes, and although these may, on the face of it, seem unimportant, they provide context, pace and tone to an evening and can seriously affect a play's dramatic flow. Often they are an extension of a scene or even a commentary on that scene. You should consider structuring good scene changes and composing for them as an art form in itself. A decent director will not overlook their importance.

The Stylistic Function of a Score

In some plays, the function of the music is to suggest a particular period. If, for example, you are scoring a play set in Victorian London you may wish to look at the kind of music associated with the specific area in which it's set and the social class of the characters. In this instance, there will be a plethora of different musical genres including music hall, operetta, Romantic-era music and so on to look at. You'll notice the similarities and differences between music for the upper classes and music heard in the street. You'll discover a world of barrel organs on street corners, orchestras in band stands augmented by colossal additional brass forces, classical repertoire in concert halls, operas, ballets and, of course, recitals in drawing rooms and the wildly popular homespun 'piano in the parlour'. The style of music you choose to employ will be dependent on its purpose in augmenting the story.

Sometimes the guiding principle for a score will be tone. If the overarching location or time period does not feel like a vital element to latch on to with your score, you may write music that prepares the audience for the attitude of the play. Instead of trying to evoke a period or style, you may be teeing up the audience for the play's swing – setting the tone and mood. Often scores for comedies function by this approach.

You may not want to lead the audience's expectations by being too literal with the musical style. Ambiguity can be a useful tool, but bear in mind that if there's going to be music, it's going to have to be 'something'. If the requirements of the score are unclear, sometimes you can feel that the score needs to do 'everything and nothing'. It's worth remembering that fundamentally music is binary. It's either there or it isn't. It can be so quiet it's nearly imperceptible, but it's still there. Be careful as a composer not to try and sit in a middle ground that doesn't exist. Be brave and be bold and commit to your choices. This might even mean doing less rather than more.

You may come across a situation where music feels like it should emanate from character rather than geography or historical context. (See the later case study on *Strange Interlude*.) It can be better to frame the drama inherent in a character's situation and the choices they make, rather than *musically* to paint the room they make those choices in. This approach opens the doors to a huge variety of styles that may have little or nothing to do with traditionally accurate music of the time period, but can bring your score much closer to the moving line of the narrative.

And sometimes you will be scoring action. The music will reference the actual movement on stage. How this music functions stylistically will depend on the decisions you made earlier in terms of period, tone and character, but it's a good rule to try and make each element of your score sit in the same sound world or palette. Your palette can be incredibly eclectic if appropriate, or occasionally you may find yourself consciously subverting it, but it's important to maintain control of these decisions so that your score hangs together when the show runs in its entirety. Sometimes this is about reprising melodic or harmonic themes across various styles or arrangements or it can be something as simple as maintaining your instrument choices throughout. More on this later.

Often your musical goalposts will change considerably during rehearsals, and particularly during the technical rehearsal and previews. You will need to be prepared to make big adjustments. If you have a strong musical concept and you understand why you've made the decisions you have so far, it will make revisions easier to implement in a way that complements the entire score. Of course, you may find that your concept doesn't hold up in the ever-changing nature of rehearsals so you must be prepared to completely rethink everything. Try to get in the habit of stepping back from the work and looking at it objectively. Does the music fit and serve the production? Is the musical story clear? It's important to realise when your concept is worth persevering with (or even fighting for) and when you need to go in a new direction and quickly. As the theatre director Simon Godwin helpfully said to me once: 'Hold on tightly, let go lightly.'

Diegetic and Non-diegetic Music

Plays will often call for specific pieces of music to be used as part of a scene – a common example is a radio playing onstage. When a character is *aware* of music or if it exists in their world it is termed 'diegetic'. This is the case most commonly when music is written into a play. Conversely, when music exists outside the world of the play – often scene-change music or underscoring, and the characters are *unaware* of the music – it is known as 'non-diegetic'. From a practical standpoint it is important to note the difference between these two for, as we will learn later, it impacts rights issues and budgets.

Pre-production Work with the Director

The relationship with the director is one of the most important ones you'll forge in the theatre. He is the person who will marshal the production towards a seamless, integrated whole. He is also the person who will get you hired. Creatively, a director is in charge and will expect you to work with him to realise a collective objective for the project.

At your first creative meeting (which may be in addition to any preliminary meetings) the director will expect you to have read the play and have an initial gut response, but more importantly this is an opportunity for him to share his thoughts. It is normally the case that he will already have had many meetings with the set designer and it's likely they have a model box of the set to show you. Use this meeting as an opportunity to try and understand the nature, style and ambition of the production. Every process is different, but sometimes the whole creative team will meet early on to look at the model box together. Regularly this will include the director, the set designer, the lighting designer, the composer, the sound designer, the costume designer (if different to the set designer) and possibly the movement director. This gives you a chance to ask open questions about the fundamental concept and set design, and how every department will tie in to create a cohesive whole.

You can ask questions on scale, theatrical design, layout, audience size and orientation, and how the director intends the creative process to develop. It can be useful to suggest musical styles at this stage, but don't tie yourself down or make any concrete choices. There is normally time during the rehearsal process to make compositional decisions once you've heard the play spoken out loud; it can be especially useful to see it on its feet. Very occasionally, however, you will have to turn up on day one of rehearsals with music for the actors to learn. Every process is different, but this creative meeting will help inform you further as to what is expected ahead of time.

Vision

Quite often, when mounting a play, and especially when mounting a classic, directors will be expected to bring a new idea to the table, or have a new 'take'. Even if it's a Shakespeare play and they decide to try to replicate a period production, this is still a choice, and will involve great imagination to make it work effectively. Whatever decisions are made in this respect it's important to remember that *everything is a choice*. Directors constantly have to answer questions on every aspect of a production from set to costumes, to lighting to music and so on. Each element of a production is created by someone to fulfil a purpose and a director can't be there to oversee every moment of creation. It's important therefore to understand – to the extent it's possible during the production process, and knowing it might change – what it is you're aiming for.

Shakespeare's work is probably the most enduring of any classical writer and, more than any of the other plays in the classical canon, can inspire and withstand bold new interpretations. Sometimes a play will be re-imagined in a fundamental way, as part of a director's 'take', but these decisions will never be entered into lightly. It has become increasingly common to 'update' Shakespeare by setting the plays in altered locations and periods, but these will never (in theory) be arbitrary choices. The hope is always that by changing the context of these plays, something fresh and original will be discovered, or that the themes they explore will be highlighted in an effective or even newly enlightened way. The reasoning behind a director's choice as to a production's interpretation and setting will affect everything you do musically. A common joke I come across when discussing new 'takes' on classic plays (which is never popular with directors, by the way), is when someone asks: 'Are we going to set it on a spaceship?'

Despite all this talk about 'takes', however, theatre is at its heart about collaboration. Some directors dislike the idea of their having a 'vision' as it implies they are expected to have imagined all the problems and solutions before the process starts. Besides being a trifle unrealistic, this would basically render the rehearsal process and the actors' contribution void, and discount the happy accidents, discoveries and insights that occur when a group of talented people strive to achieve a collective creative ambition. A good theatre director will have an idea of what he wants to achieve, but will utilise the talents of his creative team and actors to shape a united whole. Sometimes the word 'vision' is used in a negative context when people either don't understand or agree with a director's choices. They blame it on the director's 'vision'.

I have also heard a director (perhaps rather reservedly) say that he surrounds himself with people who are 'individually much better at their jobs' than he is, and that he feels like the least talented person in the room. I believe what he means is that each member of the creative team has a more specific knowledge of their field and will have the time and energy to focus on that particular element of the production. A director will try to surround himself with people he trusts and who are experts in their disciplines, but it is he who must 'direct' and shape their contributions into a coherent production.

Research

In order to build your musical palette you will normally want to spend a significant amount of time researching: look at the period of the play, the background and style of the author and any musical influences you may feel are relevant to the story, the themes, the character and the cultural or geographical setting. You can also build up a bank of images from the period or context (paintings, illustrations, costumes, photos from other similar plays or films) or of the emotional palette or activities in the play. Perhaps you'll want to read extracts from history books, biographies, plays and poetry from the time. This is all part of the process of really getting into the world of the play – rather than just listening to the relevant music. Normally the first part of the rehearsal process with the acting company is all about this kind of research so you may want to make yourself available for those sessions. (More on this later.) As technology becomes more and more advanced and possibilities for information and music sharing increase, we are blessed with an almost inexhaustible reference tool in the internet, but this should not stop you from looking in other, more traditional outlets.

As part of your music research, a traditional music library (if you have access to one) is a veritable treasure trove of old orchestral scores, books of old songs, books on theory and history of music, and archived recordings that will never make it to online release. Although a lot of information is now stored online, there's nothing quite like standing in a library surrounded by your musical heritage. It's important to respect and learn from what has come before. Don't, however, allow yourself to feel constricted by the rulebooks and the layouts of other music. If you are employed as the composer for a show, take heart that the director trusts in your ability to create new music that can be influenced and informed, but not hemmed in by stylistic choices of the past.

Take into consideration the function of music from a specific period. Begin by looking at the time in which it was written: the cultural climate, why a composer was writing this music and for whom. Look at what else was in vogue at the time. Where does a composer hail from geographically and where are they writing? Who was playing the music? Why did they play it? Where did they play it? Who was listening? Who wasn't listening and why? Was it written down? How was it passed from generation to generation? What musical influences inspired it? What instruments were being played? Was it considered good at the time? Was it popular? Where did the music sit in terms of the tiers of the social class system? How was it shared?

When you start to answer these questions (and a world of others that will undoubtedly become relevant, sometimes via a director's suggestion), you'll hopefully get a more in-depth impression of how the music of that period worked. In a later chapter we will contemplate melodic and harmonic choices composers make and how these inform their style. All of these elements are useful tools to utilise when writing new music influenced by another time and place.

Writing Blind

One of the most challenging things about writing music for theatre is that you don't get to see the image that the audience will see (particularly in a scene change) at the time you're composing. So much of theatre composition is about tone, which is something you might not get a handle on until you see the whole play run together on set and in costume. In film you can mostly score to picture, so you can hope to get a sense of how the music fits. In the theatre it often feels like you're writing blind and hoping that when you come to combine all the disparate elements of design, lighting, sound, actors and costume that each creative aspect will feel part of the same production. This is why it is so important to understand what every department is doing and observe as much of a rehearsal process as possible. A scene change can be purely about a shift in time, or a few incidental props changing, or it can have a fully realised dramatic narrative.

These big, narrative scene changes are the hardest to imagine at the writing stage, because no matter how well they are pre-planned or storyboarded, you won't really know how they work practically until you get into the theatre at the technical rehearsal. You must prepare yourself for many eventualities, normally by writing several variations and alternatives for each cue.

Content Dictates Form

In musical theatre, a mantra often cited (most famously by Stephen Sondheim) is that 'content dictates form'. This applies to the way in which songs and musical choices are bred from the text; it is equally applicable to the play. Often bad (or inappropriate) score writing in plays will come from a composer's desire to write a specific type of cue that they have been mulling over either consciously or subconsciously for some time, or an initial idea they cannot let go. This can be a problem that arises from thinking too much about a project too prematurely in the process. It's great to come prepared with lots of ideas and examples of pre-existing music to show-and-tell, but you must make sure that you don't go too far down a certain road on your own before taking the other creative areas of the production into consideration.

Form Informs Form

If you keep informed of what the other departments are aiming at, hopefully you'll be on the same page as the director and the rest of the creative team. This is not to say that certain ideas will be wrong, or that occasional wildcard suggestions may not lead to something wholly unexpected and wonderful. In time you may end up going in a completely different direction from what you first thought or agreed on, and sometimes a director will be thrilled to have a suggestion come out of left field. Lots of new information and ideas will come out of rehearsals, technical rehearsals and previews. Your original musical concept might shift completely in a direction no one anticipated. Sometimes it can even be a good idea to consider the complete antithesis to what you originally had in mind for a cue. If anything, it will help to keep your approach creatively supple. The important thing, especially at the pre-rehearsal and early rehearsal stage, is to keep your options open.

Creating a Sound World

One of the most important things you need to consider at the beginning of your planning process (and keep referring to and honing over time) is how you'll define the 'sound world' of your production. What will you make Tudor London, early twentieth-century New England or 1980s Gibraltar sound like? It relates to all sound effects and, of course, instrument choices and musical cues. It's worth looking at how characters relate to their surroundings and how the setting affects the dramatic arc of the play. It can even be worth listening out for accent choices or indeed anything that is particular to the area in which it's set. What you're striving to create is a seamless, appropriate (to the concept and world of the production) sound score that pulls the separate elements of music and sound design into a cohesive whole. It is about ensuring consistency across all elements in sound/music so that nothing jars with or falls outside the world you are trying to create. This is an important area in which you'll want to be working closely with the sound designer.

Sound Designers

Early in the production process, hopefully pre-production, you will meet the sound designer. Next to the director, this is the person with whom you will work most closely in the theatre. There is a chapter on working with the sound designer later in this book, but as we're currently addressing the pre-production process, one of the first things you should discuss with them (besides your understanding of the play) is what you hope to accomplish musically and how you intend to do it.

They will work through the practicalities of making your ambition a reality and their input can affect the way you approach your composition on a rudimentary level. Sometimes a reality check is in order, but as in all creative processes try not to let the limitations of technology get in your way at this stage. It's far better to keep an open mind and each other informed. With time, over the rehearsal period, you will start to focus on exactly how the music will function and pare down your ideas. The sound designer will help you get there in practical terms. In the same way that having a close relationship with a director and designer will help you create a piece that blends all disciplines into one show, you should be aware of the needs of a sound designer, how they will make their choices, and how you can help them by keeping them abreast of your composition process. It goes without saying that you should view this relationship as a collaboration rather than technical support.

Sound effects, which typically sit in the sound designer's domain, may spark your interest, though it is normally the sound designer's job to source them. This is not to say that you cannot help or suggest ideas. Depending on your relationship, the lines may become blurred between what is composition and what is sound design. There are a growing number of people who do both jobs at once (more on that later). The sound world of the play as a whole is something both the composer and the sound designer are collectively responsible for.

Case Study: *The Recruiting Officer* at the Donmar Warehouse

The Play

The Recruiting Officer by George Farquhar is a Restoration comedy, which was first staged at the Theatre Royal Drury Lane in 1706. The Donmar Warehouse produced a revival in 2012 as Josie Rourke's inaugural production as artistic director. It tells the story of recruiting sergeant Captain Plume and his sidekick Sergeant Kite, who descend upon the country town of Shrewsbury with the ambition to recruit the local men to the army. In turn, they rekindle old loves and stir up chaos along the way. It's a play full of mistaken identity, tawdry love matches, double-dealing and cross-dressing, but as a piece of Restoration comedy it possesses a rare humanity uncommon in many of the more brittle, high-society plays of the genre.

The Approach

The Recruiting Officer is quite regularly presented with the musical score weighted towards the military aspects of the story, but after our initial meetings we decided it would be musically interesting to trace a journey charting how a rural naivety could become corrupted by the presence of the military. Although for the most part it is a light and airy comedy, we found there to be a serious and wistful undercurrent present throughout the play – that of the realities of war. In the action of the play, by coercion and trickery, the military men force the country folk to abandon their rural ideals and head off to battle to die for their country. We decided therefore that alongside the military music (which is partly written into the play) we would shift the focus to period-inspired folk music and observe how these extrinsic forces acted upon it.

The Design

Looking at the model box and discussing the design ideas, it was clear that conceptually the director, Josie Rourke, and the designer, Lucy Osborne, had imagined the Donmar space much closer to the building's origins as a warehouse. Part of their brief to the team as a whole was to try and evoke how an acting company of the early eighteenth century might have staged the play. The auditorium layout of the Donmar is typically audience on three sides on two levels around a thrust stage. In this design, there were two wooden 'perch' areas at balcony level upstage right and left, with staircases leading to each. These were positioned above an open raked wooden stage and a concertinaed backdrop of a painted sky lit by dozens of candles. There were also candlelit chandeliers and candle-like lamps around the rim of the circle. The idea was to make the entire stage feel like it was lit by warm candlelight and this fitted well with the unaffected rural earthiness of folk music. The perches were designed to house a band of actor-musicians split across the two sides, the idea being that these actors would play various parts in the show whilst also providing the musical accompaniment for songs, underscore and scene changes. They would also play twenty minutes or so of pre-show music as the audience entered to establish the musical world of the play and give the entire space an eighteenth-century, warm and welcoming ambience from the off.

The Research

Having first been performed in 1706, there were mentions in the script of songs that have since been lost. Alongside those there were references to military marches of the day, some of which are still in commonplace use. I found a couple of melodies for the more obscure songs that had survived in lead-sheet form, but we decided early on that the two most famous pieces of music, 'The Grenadier March' and 'Over the Hills and Far Away' were the only originals we would use. I would write new musical settings for any other existing lyrics and compose brand new music everywhere else. This allowed me to write music specifically in terms of style, tone and function for scenes in this particular production (which was, as is common in many revivals of old plays, lovingly adapted from the original), rather than adapt something pre-existing to fit. In any case, it was a fun challenge to write some site-specific and character-specific folk songs and dances.

I started by looking at a variety of folk music from the late seventeenth and early eighteenth centuries. Initially I looked at mostly English references, but also bits of Celtic and Eastern European music came in useful. Folk music tends to be less well documented than the classical repertoire. We know it was passed down orally through generations or sometimes scrawled down, mostly as melody lines. The most useful reference I found was *The Dancing Master*, which is a collection of instructions and single line melodies to teach set English country dances. As it's still in common use today, some modern-day recordings of these pieces also exist.

When looking at modern-day recordings or interpretations of period music, be aware that (in the same way that musicians in the original period would have done) contemporary players will make (often unconscious) musical choices they assimilate from their own background or cultural environment. Of course, some ensembles make a point of deliberately trying to recreate an authentic sound, but it may be that the manner in which they play and the instruments they use may be of a slightly different nature to those authentically of the period (especially if we're looking at folk music). It's likely you'll want to rework any style references to fit within your particular aesthetic anyway, but don't imagine every recording you hear to be the 'real deal'.

When doing research into the history of music it is important to consider that all live music is relative to its environment. You should consider the expectations of an audience both today and in the period in which the music originally existed. With eighteenth-century folk music, we can quite readily assume that the audience were there primarily to dance, so music served as a rhythm and structure to keep the dance going. An eighteenth-century audience would have had a different relationship to the quality of the sound than a modern one accustomed to amplification. Concert halls were built to house professional ensembles and orchestras, and were acoustically designed for that purpose; a folk-band playing for a dance in a rural part of England would not have had the same luxury. That's not to say you should spend all of your time trying faithfully to replicate an inferior instrument quality to be 'authentic', but it's an interesting part of the research to bear in mind.

When making decisions on musical content and style it's incredibly useful to be able to play references to a director to get their feedback. When an author doesn't have a specific musical style in mind it'll be up to you to suggest your own ideas. It can be particularly useful to generate more than one stylistic idea; sometimes contrasting forms combined will produce something new and unique for your production.

The Musicians

The practicality of the way the actor-musician band would act as both characters in *The Recruiting Officer* and the musical accompaniment also affected the way in which I thought about the score, making sure in every moment we had the necessary combination of instruments available to fill the space. From discussions with the director, which included budgetary constraints alongside artistic ideals, it became apparent that we could use up to five actor-musicians.

When looking at your instrument line-up, remember that your job as a composer for the modern theatre is not to create a museum piece (although that can sometimes happen), but to serve the production that you are writing for. Because of this you may have to compromise on what is historically accurate.

In a later chapter we will look in more detail at the reasoning behind the instrument line-up for *The Recruiting Officer*, but for now let's accept that we had a five-piece band consisting of military snare/side drum, upright bass, acoustic guitar, violin and flute/tin-whistle. All of the instrumentalists would sing live and be subtly mic'd.

Music Spotting

Having looked a bit more at the history of folk music and listened to modern interpretations of the music of the period, it was time to sit down with the director and methodically go through the script to place the music or 'music spot'. This production consisted of lots of short scenes across numerous locations, so the call for scene-change and scene-setting music was a significant one. Due to the nature of the design, the physical set would not change greatly from scene to scene, nor would there be (aside from a few big set-piece scene changes) any recurrent shifting of furniture or props. Bear in mind also that the concept of the lighting design was that the whole space would feel as if it were lit by candlelight. This meant the way each scene looked wouldn't necessarily indicate big changes in time and location (as it normally might do), leaving space for the music to accomplish changes of setting and mood. Together, Josie Rourke and I went through the play and marked the points where music might fit, and noted what each scene change needed to accomplish both dramatically and practically (as far as was possible at that stage). From my research we also had at our disposal several excerpt recordings of folk music we could use almost as a temp score.

In film, a 'temp score' is a temporary score of pre-existing music that is synced to the picture to give a sense of tone, feel and tempo before any new music is written. It is then replaced with original music at a later point. Similarly, you can use it as a placeholder in the theatre.

We began to create a musical palette informed by the script and to imagine a very loose staging alongside the music. This is an example of the sort of notes I would make:

> Violin (perhaps accompanied by guitar) starts playing something soft and romantic to frame the mood at the end of the scene, the drums then kick in with a contrasting military feel and take over as the scene change proper starts. As the focus on stage shifts, the other instruments then join to build and fill out the sound. All instruments except for drums then cut out, and the drums complete a military snare pattern buttoning us into the next scene.

A 'button' is essentially an accent that marks the end of a piece of music as definite. Buttoning is useful for snappy pick-ups into scenes or clear endings when you want to allow for a moment of applause. More on this later.

Another example from my *Recruiting Officer* notes looks like this:

> We begin in a place of high romanticism, fracture through a military presence and end up back in the countryside which has become somewhat flavoured by the harshness of the military.

A bit pretentious and somewhat vague perhaps, but it gave me a clear indication of the proposed structure and what needed to be accomplished sonically. How to achieve this is something to be worked out when you sit down to write. At this stage it is about ideas; you don't need to worry about exactly what the notes will be.

For each scene change I would track the tonal passing of the story from the previous scene into the new one, meanwhile tracing the overall musical arc of the evening. I wanted the score to mature as the play progressed so that by the end the music would have developed and mirrored the dramatic journey of the play. We were also keen to mine the vast variety in music around this period, which allowed us to widen our musical palette and take the audience on a fully realised sonic tour. For example, we came across some beautiful a cappella songs (historically known as 'Glees') featuring a counter-tenor lead. These evoked a completely different mood and feel altogether from the boisterous folk style we'd already utilised. Glees are not technically classed as 'folk music' but, of course, the trick is to incorporate these ideas seamlessly so that they all form part of the same musical world (however expansive that might become). Also, new ideas will always develop in the rehearsal room once the play is on its feet.

Working through the play and making notes of what we thought each scene change would need to achieve, we also spotted moments where we thought we could include new songs. We decided to find appropriate period poetry that seemed to fit the purpose of the scene for which I would compose new musical settings. (We will cover finding, writing and setting lyrics later.)

One of the major plot points in the play is the desire of the visiting sergeants to recruit the country folk to the army. The methods they used, though incredibly diverse, frequently made use of the song 'Over the Hills and Far Away' which has famously been used as a recruitment ballad for centuries. Thematically we wanted to incorporate this song into the show. After watching these rural men be duped into joining the army, we felt there was a convincing case to end the production with a coda where we would see the five actor-musicians (who had been playing various roles throughout) to play one final song together before marching off to war and (most probably) dying for their country. This would be the moment to include the full version of 'Over the Hills and Far Away'. By leaving this moment to the very end of the play, musically speaking, we had built enough tension to earn it in its entirety and provide a contrasting yet fitting end to a story that could have been played purely for its frivolity.

Different Strokes for Different Folks

The preliminary pre-production meeting with the director (if you have this meeting at all) will not always be as involved or detailed as with *The Recruiting Officer*. This was an exceptional case in terms of how the music became integral to the theatrical telling of the play. Music often supports the dramatic function of the text, but in this case it could be argued that it provided part of the narrative drive. It's also worth remembering that a large proportion of the cast were going to be actor-musicians and all the music would be played live. As a result, I needed to have a relatively clear vision of the music quite early in the process to ensure the music was a core part of the narrative from the start, and to give the actor-musicians material to work with throughout rehearsals. Typically, you won't be expected to get a complete handle on how the music will function until well into the rehearsal process, because the music usually needs to fit around the emerging production.

Remember that each director will work differently and each show will be tackled in a different manner. If you have built a relationship with a director over time and several productions, it may be that you don't need to have this meeting, especially if the musical aspects of the production are not thought to be large in scope. Sometimes I have met with a director on the first day of rehearsals and they have simply asked me what I had in mind musically. At that stage a quick answer in terms of style and function sufficed. Every situation will be different.

The Sound World

With *The Recruiting Officer* the sound brief was to make the entire world of the production feel organic and rustic. We wanted to present the play as a theatre company in the early eighteenth century might have done. This meant that there should be no trace of electronic help through amplification or pre-recorded sound. If there were to be sound effects of a rainstorm, for example, these would be achieved through traditional foley (sound-effect) techniques such as thunder sheets and 'dried peas in a drum', rather than recorded sound effects playing through a discernible PA system. In the end, most of the foley wasn't needed, but I have used similar techniques in other productions. Emma Laxton, who was the sound designer on this production, managed to make it appear to the audience as if there had been no sound designer at all. All the instruments and singers were mic'd and enhanced through a hidden sound system, but in such a subtle way that you could never consider there had been any enhancement. This is especially important in plays as actors tend not to be mic'd, and there exists a gulf between the acoustic capacities of the human voice and the extreme volume level you can reach with a theatrical sound system. In this show the key was subtly to extend all acoustic capabilities rather than over-amplify them. Passing by unnoticed in this production was the mark of an excellent sound design.

Being Prepared

With *The Recruiting Officer*, I turned up on day one of rehearsals with an entire bundle of sheet music to teach to and rehearse with the band. We spent much of the first two weeks of our five-week rehearsal period in a separate music studio learning and developing the score. We would then gradually drip-feed music into the main rehearsal room and into the play proper as rehearsals progressed. I'd edit or score new pieces as we found out what worked and what didn't, rewrite overnight and come in the next day to rehearse anew. This is a labour-intensive way to work and may initially sound rather daunting, but it's fascinating and thrilling to see a play come to life in this way.

One of my favourite moments as a composer is when an acting company first engages with the music. When the parts of the puzzle start to slot into each other and you see where you're headed, it's not only exciting, but very useful preparation for the music you've yet to write. You can then tailor brand new cues towards the final production as it evolves. Sometimes you discover what you've written doesn't work, but one of the joys of composition is that it's not a finite resource. If something you've written isn't right, get redrafting, or throw it out and write something else; but always make sure you understand why a cue doesn't work.

Absorb. Learn. Rewrite.

New Plays and Revivals

As we know, it's a good idea to do some wider general research about a play and perhaps any previous productions that have been staged. If you're working on a revival of a play there's a chance that a record will exist of those productions. It's uncommon that the music from a play will be recorded and released, although not unheard of, but there may very well be reviews that mention the use of music, or even just generally the style and tone of the production.

The Royal Shakespeare Company have made a point of recording albums of their recent Shakespeare shows. On some of these albums they've also included new recordings of music from previous productions, some going back nearly eighty years. My recording of *The Two Gentlemen of Verona* also includes excerpts from Anthony Bernard's score from the 1938 production. It's fascinating to listen to how different composers have approached the same material in different eras in what are clearly wildly different productions.

Personally I don't spend much time looking at what other productions have done musically, I'd rather start my process with the text and do my own research. As with everything in the creative process, there are no set rules. Every composer works differently. I like to sit with the play and my research for a while and get a gut feeling for how I think the show should sound. This is usually a good enough starting place to at least have a conversation with the director.

With a new play you should start by approaching the text in exactly the same way as you would with a classic. You should be able to ascertain useful clues about potential musical form and style from the dialogue and instructions the writer provides. If you are fortunate enough to have the writer in the room with you, you can ask them directly what they envision for the sound score. Some writers are more forthcoming with their music ideas than others. It's always very useful to get an insight because they will almost always have had some kind of idea in mind. This doesn't mean you shouldn't suggest completely new ideas that you take from the text. Bear in mind that music is your area of expertise and most writers will be interested to hear your thoughts. Ultimately, it is the director's call which direction the music goes in, but hopefully everyone will end up on the same page.

Case Study: The Worries of a Playwright

I was once asked to compose the score for a new play and on the first day the writer gave me a piece of music he had been listening to whilst he had been writing. This music was what he anticipated the score would sound like. Listening to it, and after reading the play, I could see why he was attached to it, but also that in a theatrical context it wouldn't fully serve the piece on stage. This piece of music was intended as a tonal guide, rather than a fully-fledged attempt at a score, but it turned out he had become more attached to it than perhaps was useful. A score for a play needs to develop as the narrative does. You shouldn't limit yourself to the same piece of music for every scene change (unless it's for a very specific reason) as it will become predictable and boring for an audience and ultimately it won't serve the dramatic arc. It was very useful to hear where he located the sound world from this music, but I was aware that I would have to write something original that incorporated these stylistic ideas whilst tracking a journey through the piece.

When I played my first draft to the director, he was very enthusiastic and said it fitted very well, but when the writer came to a runthrough and heard it for the first time he was less enthusiastic. This became a bit of an odd situation as the director then backtracked out of respect for the writer, and I was asked to redraft. In hindsight, the music for this particular new play wasn't far off in terms of structure; it just needed a nudge in a slightly different stylistic direction. However, because the writer had the original piece of music so solidly ingrained in his mind, it took more than a few drafts to gain his approval.

Getting It Wrong

The entire rehearsal process is built around experimentation with ideas and you should remain open to that like everyone else. Often you won't 'nail it' on a first draft and you may have to come up with an alternative very quickly. It doesn't necessarily have to be the final polished draft at that stage, but it needs to evoke what that final cue could be. I've thrown complete scores out in the final week of rehearsal and rewritten them when we eventually put all the scenes together and did a run. It's completely normal practice to be redrafting and editing music in the technical rehearsal, because sometimes it's only once you're in the theatre, looking at the actual set, that you begin to see what is really required. Also, if you've written a piece of music to cover a scene change, it doesn't matter how often you rehearse it beforehand, the timings will always alter (sometimes drastically) when you're in the theatre proper.

Although at times it may seem harsh, you should try not to let a director's notes or criticism affect you on a personal level. This can be a hard lesson to learn, but it's part of the process of being a theatre composer. Notes are about making 'the work' better. Although it may sometimes seem difficult to discern the difference between you and your work, it's helpful to remind yourself that ultimately once the music is created, it exists as an entity in itself. It is written to serve a purpose – any notes given will hopefully help it to achieve that purpose to its maximum capacity. Always remember that everyone is working towards a mutual goal: to serve the play. Sometimes you will nail a score on a first go and receive almost no notes. An achievement though this is, and I have to say relatively uncommon, it can somehow leave you feeling less satisfied with the final result. Theatre is a collaborative form and, in a way, notes are a way of a director or writer engaging with your work. Happily though, if you come prepared and leave your ego at the door, it's likely you will come out of every process having learned something useful. At the end of the day you'll (hopefully) have usefully 'added' to the production and created something that didn't exist before. There's a real achievement in that.

When to Compose

Deciding when to start your actual composing will depend very much on the function of the music in the production. If you're writing mostly scene-change music and it's a recorded score, generally I'd suggest you start by sketching out ideas in the early weeks of rehearsal but don't settle on anything until the last week – unless, of course, cues are needed in the rehearsal room earlier. Changes occur so frequently with theatre productions that you need to be able to move with them and not get too absorbed in an out-of-date score.

Most directors will want to hear at least a simple demo before you record the score proper and you might find that listening to it together sparks a creative idea or two. This is also a necessary part of the process for your own peace of mind as you can hopefully come away from that meeting knowing that you're on the right track. If a director trusts you and knows you will deliver, they may be fine to leave you to your own schedule, but I'd suggest you always keep them abreast of what you're doing. You wouldn't want to record a score that's not what they want or thought they had agreed to.

Most of your time spent during rehearsals will be about deciding what to write. All the information and influences you take from your meetings and all the research you do will constantly be whirring about in both your conscious and subconscious mind. If you can sit in on rehearsals, even better, as you'll start to absorb the influence of the actors and the director-in-process and begin to assimilate ideas. Even if you don't feel like you're doing anything productive during the rehearsal period, it's most likely that via time and osmosis, your brain will be working it out. I normally find that with the pressure of a deadline looming and the combined experiences of the rehearsal room and creative meetings, when I finally get down to the actual writing in the latter stages of rehearsals it happens relatively quickly.

Being prepared to (and able to) work fast has often held me in good stead. The first production I scored for the National Theatre came about because the original composer dropped out at the end of the last week of rehearsals. I was very quickly drafted in and introduced to the creative team, cast and production. The timeline looked like this:

> On Friday afternoon I received a phone call and was asked to come to the rehearsal room; I caught the end of rehearsals.
>
> On Friday evening I met with the director, the designer and the head of music and was officially offered the job.
>
> On Saturday morning I watched a run of the play (having had no time to read it) and had to decide which instruments I wished to record. The session musicians were then booked for the Monday.

> On Saturday evening I did some research into the period and the style of music we were looking at.
>
> On Sunday I wrote the entire score.
>
> On Monday I recorded it.
>
> On Tuesday I played it to the director, received some notes and mixed it.
>
> On Wednesday we began the technical rehearsal.

This seems extreme in terms of the timescale, but it's not unheard of. This show wasn't a small amount of music either, but quite often if it is (and in normal circumstances), I won't actually write the score until very late in the process.

Once you understand what the music needs to achieve and how it will function as part of the production, the act of writing is applying the research; craft; and getting through it all.

If you go to your piano/desk/pencil/laptop prepared with a good knowledge of the play, and you understand to the best of your ability the tone and style, and you've made a good guide as to what needs to be accomplished, you'll never be sitting down at a completely blank piece of paper. Not for long anyway.

Research and preparation are some of the best ways to combat writer's block and hopefully keep you from feeling isolated.

A play is produced by many people combined, but at some point it is you who will have to create the music, play it to the director and let the company hear it for the first time. These moments are always terrifying and exhilarating in equal measure, no matter what level you're at.

Act Two:
Composition

'Without craftsmanship,
inspiration is a mere reed
shaken in the wind.'

Johannes Brahms

Creating a Musical World

The Power of Sound

Music is unique as an art form in that it elicits a visceral response from the listener that requires next to no effort on his or her own part. If you're looking at a painting or film, or reading a passage in a novel, it is possible you may not fully comprehend it, or you may switch off and not absorb it at all. Sometimes you can simply not be seeing what the artist wishes you to look at. Hearing, however, you cannot turn off. I've always been fascinated by the instinctive response people have to sound, and the tools this provides to us as composers.

We've all been in a situation where a sudden loud noise made us jump. If we happen to be in the vicinity of the noise, it's not possible that we could be simply 'hearing the wrong way'. We don't need to be concentrating on the sound for it to scare us. What commonly occurs after a shock like this is that a part of our brain known as the hypothalamus initiates a 'sequence of nerve-cell firing and chemical release... chemicals like adrenaline, noradrenaline and cortisol are released into our bloodstream'[11] which prepares our body for running or fighting. This creates a prickly sensation across our skin, heightens our other senses, diminishes our perception of pain and leads to an increase in our heart rate. The 'fight or flight' principle is a primitive, in-built self-defence mechanism gifted to us by Mother Nature and evolution to help preserve our species. If a listener actively engages in the sounds around them they can begin to appreciate the nuance of a sound and contextualise it to an extent, but they are powerless to remain unaffected at all.

The point here is that as a 'sound creator' – a composer or sound designer – you have at your disposal an uncommon amount of power over a group of people. You can shock people, scare people, unnerve people, move people, even sicken people with sound. How many of us are unable to deal with even the thought of fingernails being drawn across a blackboard? Some sounds can be designed to provoke a physical reaction from an audience. Daft as it may sound, writing music or creating sound for a public performance comes with a certain amount of responsibility.

Case Study: Infrasound

Infrasound or 'low-frequency sound' is defined as 'sound waves below the frequencies of audible sound, and nominally includes anything under 20Hz'.[12] Infrasound is felt rather than heard. Gerry Vassilatos wrote in a paper for the *Journal of Borderland Research* that 'Infrasound produces varied physiological sensations that begin as vague "irritations". At certain pitch, infrasound produces physical pressure. At specific low intensity, fear and disorientation. Nazi propaganda engineers methodically used infrasound to stir up the hostilities of crowds who were gathered to hear [Hitler].'[13]

Infrasound can occur in nature, caused by extreme weather, seismic tremors or even by animals such as elephants, giraffes and whales who use it to communicate or ward off foes.[14]

Infrasonic waves are known to cause feelings of nausea, in-ear pressure and in some cases terror, nausea and dread.[15] In his book, *Lost Science*, Gerry Vassilatos references an unlikely victim of this phenomenon:

> Walt Disney and his artists were once made seriously ill when a sound effect, intended for a short cartoon scene, was slowed down several times on a tape

> machine and amplified through a theatre sound system. The original sound source was a soldering iron, whose buzzing 60-cycle tone was lowered five times to 12 cycles. This tone produced a lingering nausea in the crew which lasted for days.[16]

A paper published by Vic Tandy entitled 'The Case of the Ghost in the Machine' concerns the psychological effects of infrasound. Tandy was an engineering designer who worked for a company manufacturing medical equipment. He started (along with his colleagues) to notice 'a feeling of depression, occasionally a cold shiver... a growing level of discomfort'. One evening, when he was on his own in the laboratory, in the centre of the room, 'he became aware that he was being watched, and a figure slowly emerged to his left. It was indistinct and on the periphery of his vision but it moved as Tandy would expect a person to. The apparition was grey and made no sound. The hair was standing up on his neck and there was a distinct chill in the room. As he recalls, "It would not be unreasonable to suggest I was terrified." He was unable to see any detail and finally built up the courage to turn and face the thing. As he turned the apparition faded and disappeared.'

By a stroke of good fortune and clever engineering he discovered that the cause of this was a low-frequency standing wave caused by a fan in the extraction system. The dimensions of the room and the length of the wave meant the energy focused in the spot he was sitting. He found out that the frequency at which it resonated interacted with the frequencies at which his head and eyes naturally resonate causing discomfort and blurry vision. The fan was modified and the nausea and ghost vanished.[17]

In 2003, Jonathan Amos from the BBC wrote an interesting article that suggested that 'people who experience a sense of spirituality in church may be reacting to the extreme bass sound produced by some organ pipes'.[18]

An experiment by Professor Richard Wiseman from the University of Hertfordshire played a piece of contemporary music laced with intermittent infrasonic sound to an audience of 750 people. The results showed that 'odd sensations in the audience increased by an average of 22% when the extreme bass was present'. He detailed some audience reactions as being 'shivering on my wrist, an odd feeling in my stomach, increased heart rate, feeling very anxious and a sudden memory of emotional loss'.[19]

Focus and Practicality

We know that simple crude sound and physics can have a substantial effect on a listener. The composer and sound designer's job is to harness audio to better tell a story. I'm not in any way suggesting you use infrasonic waves to make a thriller scarier but the principles of 'coercion' with sound have been used in many different and (in the case of Adolf Hitler) disturbing ways.

In the theatre a large part of a director's job is telling the audience where to look and when. It is about focus. Good music and sound design work in a similar way. Underscore can add depth to a moment or highlight an action. Scene-change music creates or shifts mood and adapts the pace of an evening. Some writers (and actors) object to music and sound design as they think they 'instruct' an audience how to feel and would rather the text and performance did that. In my opinion, you can have the best of both worlds. Music and sound can be seamlessly incorporated into the narrative arc of the show, but they can be necessary for the production from a purely practical perspective. Sometimes, a scene change is required when the only alternative would be for the audience to sit in silence as stagehands noisily move furniture about. In this case it alienates an audience, makes them feel uncomfortable, awkward and ultimately ignored. Some plays don't require much in the way of underscore, but most of them require some changing of scene or location even in a minimal way.

More About Diegetic and Non-diegetic Music

Diegetic music can also be termed 'source', 'found music' or 'actual sound' and is defined as any sound or music presented as originated from a source within the story-space. It can be offstage as long as it exists within the world of the piece.

Non-diegetic music can be termed 'extra-diegetic', 'incidental', 'curtain music' or 'commentary sound' and describes music or sound that originates from outside the boundaries of the story-space. It is not present in the action of the scene. The Performing Rights Society defines this as: 'Music heard by the theatre audience as an accompaniment to the play, but which is not performed by or intended to be audible to any of the characters in the play.'[20]

Included in this category is incidental music, which is written by a composer for a specific production to enhance, focus or accompany action or mood. It can also function as transitional music (between scenes) or be used to open or close a performance.

Diegetic and non-diegetic terminology also applies to films and musical theatre. In the Baz Luhrmann film *Moulin Rouge*, the number 'Sparkling Diamonds' is diegetic as the song is part of a performance inside the narrative: Satine and the performers know they are singing. The song 'One Day I'll Fly Away' is non-diegetic as the musical element here exists outside the world of the narrative: Satine is unaware she is singing.[21]

Found Music

Within the diegetic music category, we find what is known as found or interpolated music. The Performing Rights Society defines interpolated music as: 'Music not specially written for a theatrical production (and excluding overture, entr'acte, exit, incidental and curtain music) and which is performed by or intended to be audible to a character or characters in that theatrical production.'[22] In other words, music you will not write yourself but will be part of the action in the show. We'll cover more about copyrights and licences later.

Commonly, interpolated music comes in the form of either a pre-existing and recorded song or piece of music that a character is listening to (perhaps on a radio) or a live musician, singer or band on stage. In this case, the title and perhaps even the artist is normally specified by the playwright in the script. If you're looking for a recorded piece of 'found music', there may be several options to choose from.

Case Study: *Philadelphia, Here I Come!* at the Donmar Warehouse

In the play *Philadelphia, Here I Come!* by Brian Friel, the main character, Gar, is a big fan of the Mendelssohn Violin Concerto and regularly plays it on his gramophone. The action is set in the fictional town of Ballybeg in rural Ireland in the 1960s. The Mendelssohn Violin Concerto is one of the most recorded concerti in the repertoire, but for the 2012 Donmar Warehouse production, in order to try and create a sense of authenticity, we decided to try and find a recording that could potentially have been bought in the period and location the play was set. We found an old vinyl record of the great violinist Yehudi Menuhin's recording from Abbey Road in 1958, which we believed could have found its way to rural Donegal by the 1960s. The recording has a pleasing (from an authenticity point of view) crackle and hiss, and Menuhin's individuality in phrasing is markedly unique. The result sounds stylistically different to many modern recordings. As time passes, tastes vary and different artists bring different interpretations to the same piece of music. Strangely, even though the music was originally written over a hundred years before Menuhin recorded it, the actual recording feels very much of the era in which the play was set.

Occasionally though, you may not be able to find exactly the piece of music the author was looking for, or in the case of an older play it may no longer exist. Sometimes even if you find the specified piece of music or recording it won't fit into the aesthetic of your particular production. An authentic sound cue or recording might be historically accurate, but so far from what a modern ear is accustomed to that it doesn't serve your purpose.

Case Study: *The Winslow Boy* at the Old Vic

The character of Dickie Winslow in Terence Rattigan's *The Winslow Boy* is a youthful man with a partiality for the dance trends of the day. Set sometime between 1914 and 1918 in London, there are mentions of 'the Bunny Hug', 'the Turkey Trot' and 'a Kangaroo Hop'. These are pre-war dances that were commonly performed to rag-time music. Here is a stage direction from the play:

> *He* [Arthur Winslow] *suddenly cocks his head to one side and listens. There is the sound of a gramophone playing 'Hitchy-koo' from somewhere upstairs.*

Luckily there are still recordings of this song in circulation so the task was to find one that sounded appropriate and also to choose a suitable moment in the song which would be lively and bold enough to be suitably annoying to the character of Arthur Winslow. Fortunately with this piece (being a ragtime) it begins in a lively way and continues in that vein throughout, so it was never really a challenge to find an appropriate part of the track. It's worth noting that in the world of the play the song was being played on a gramophone, so it would have been possible for it to have started playing from somewhere other than the beginning. Also, from a practical point of view, it may be necessary to repeat sections of it if the scene were to run longer than the recording. This is where (providing appropriate licences are cleared) a sound designer may need to be 'creative' with the structure of the original track.

Later in the play, references are made to 'early ragtime music' and the characters of Catherine and Dickie Winslow 'dance, in the manner of the period', but the specific tune is not indicated. In this instance the challenge is to find something appropriate to which the choreographer can choreograph a legitimate dance of the period, and something that sounds like it came from the same record collection as the guy who likes the 'Hitchy-koo' piece. In the 2013 Old Vic production it was clear to me that these should all be found pieces of music. Sometimes it's fun to write pastiches of music from a particular period, but you should only do this when your particular production renders it necessary or even possible. Most of the time in the theatre you are working to strict and limited budgets so it may be difficult to recreate the kind of music you need in full with the limited resources you have. *The Winslow Boy* still required scene-change music, however, which leads us on to non-diegetic music.

Considering Non-diegetic Music

Every theatre production will have its own requirements of non-diegetic music, but usually the most useful way to begin is by looking at the diegetic music that is already populating your story (if there is any). You may then find that you want to counter it stylistically, but in any case it's a good place to start.

Tone versus Mood

Opening music for a play tends to be about setting tone and mood. I think of 'tone' as being the writer's attitude towards the subject, and the stylistic choice evocative of a period or style. Mood is the dramatic context of the story within that tone and the atmosphere that it creates for an audience.

Tone is the approach; mood is the effect.

Evocation versus Prescription

Most of the time when composing non-diegetic music for a play, you have to focus its purpose and be economic in terms of scale, length and instrumentation. In the same way that a set design may be evocative of a location without being literal, a composition needs to evoke rather than prescribe. In a metaphorical sense I see it as presenting individual brush strokes rather than a complete colour painting. Remember that music is just one element of the production. These brush strokes exist as a part alongside the set design, lighting, costume and, of course, performances. The accumulation of all production elements needs only to add up to one complete work of art that is formed over the course of an evening.

The temptation of modern technology means that you could, without employing an orchestra, present music that is 'full to the brim' or overly cinematic in scope. I often force myself to remember the old adage of 'less is more'. The important thing to consider is balance. There are (as ever) no steadfast rules, but if a production has a small cast of four, it can feel very odd if the music is clearly being played by an ensemble of twenty. Of course, if it has been produced using software instruments rather than real ones this may not be the case, but the ear will hear it as twenty regardless. In this case, as an audience tunes in to the conventions of the evening (any opening music is likely to be the first thing they hear), they may be led along the wrong path (one of orchestral majesty) instead of one that would naturally lead to four people on a minimal set. Of course, this may be a genius move in the right context and the play may call for it, but it's worth considering if you have more instruments playing in the band than actors playing on the stage the balance might not be quite right.

Music is there to serve the play. Ideally the first line of the play should be delivered with an entire audience focused and primed. Keep space within a piece of music and allow an audience to complete the musical picture. Encourage the mind to engage and an audience will have suspended their disbelief before the curtain has fully risen.

When thinking about music for *The Winslow Boy* it became clear that as it was set in London between 1914 and 1918, and because it already featured specific references to ragtime, this would be an appropriate style in which to write (in this case, scene-change music). Aided by budget constraints I elected to write for only two instruments – a clarinet and a piano. The action of the play happens in the drawing room of an upper-middle-class house, so it seemed that too large an ensemble would be out of character with what is essentially a family drama with a small cast. A duo of clarinet and piano is more than capable of giving the feel of ragtime music but the clarinet is also adaptable enough to provide tonal pedals in and out of scenes. It is also subtle enough to morph from underscore into scene-change music in a seamless way. Using the influence of the much fuller-sounding diegetic music, I could tie the whole piece together so all the music sounded like it existed in the same world. That world doesn't have to be made up of genuine period sounds – it has to exist as its own domain as part of the form of this production.

To sum up why I thought ragtime was a suitable musical selection: there is a level of defiance in the vigour of ragtime music that resonates with the play's central themes of the underdog battling for his individual rights against the state. It also possesses a more manic energy that reflects the untamed actions of the press and enthusiastic interest of the general public in the story. If you can give a good reason why the style of music you've chosen is applicable to your story (besides being historically accurate) it will help you to focus its role as part of the overall narrative structure.

Non-diegetic Function

Every show that requires music will need it to serve a unique purpose. Are you reflecting a character's internal narrative? Are you driving the plot forward? Are you creating a mood? Are you introducing a new scene setting? Quite often it will be a case of some or all of these together. Often, music at the opening of a show tends to be about location and tone because the audience haven't met the characters yet, but the first scene may very well kick off in the middle of a piece of action and you'll need to deliver an audience to that point from the off. In short, there may be a multitude of things any one cue needs to achieve. Ideally the score should develop as the story does, so you can try to plant the seeds for development at this early stage whilst also setting the scene for the top of the play. Combining elements of time, place, tone, mood, internal and external character traits can all be useful to keep your score interesting and give it momentum.

Case Study: *Strange Interlude* at the National Theatre

When I set about writing music for the National Theatre production of *Strange Interlude* by Eugene O'Neill, it became clear that the scope of the play (in terms of character development, location and time frame) was huge. The play tells the life story of Nina Leeds, the daughter of a college professor in New England who is left traumatised by her fiancé's death in World War One. Having never been able to consummate the love affair, she becomes consumed by guilt and grief and struggles with mental illness. She is a deeply neurotic character who battles with issues of abortion, marriage, death and aging whilst striving to find 'happiness' with several men. The story moves location from houses in New England to an apartment in New York and from a luxury yacht to an antiquated pier. Sometimes there are time jumps of as many as eleven years between scenes. This is a vast canvas to work with, but most importantly, it is Nina's suffering and her absorbing and unpredictable character that fuels the drama.

The play is also notable for its extensive use of soliloquies where characters reveal their inner thoughts to the audience. This adds another level of complexity to the staging, but also highlighted to me how powerful a driving force character is in this story. Even though the music would have to convey time and location shifts, it was the tension between what characters say to each other and what they think (say in soliloquy) that would provide the jumping-off point for the score. This was a play where character led the stylistic choices of the score before location.

The dramatic turmoil of Nina's character lent a churning, melancholic quality to the score, but it still had to go a long way towards setting scene and tone outside of that. At one point there was a dramatic scene change into a New York apartment where three entire houses moved off stage to be replaced by a magnificent Art Deco staircase in a New York penthouse apartment (strikingly designed by Soutra Gilmour). This was a big change that had to inhabit Nina's forceful ambition to move forwards with her life and also track the literal moving forwards of almost eleven years. We had to introduce a new character, Gordon (Nina's son), whose childhood spanned the scene change, and also suggest the economic boom of the 1920s and the birth of many of the New York high-rises. There was also a sense within this score that it needed to sound intrinsically American, which is where listening to composers like Aaron Copland, George Gershwin and Charles Ives came in useful.

The sound designer Chris Shutt and I collaborated on blending music and sound into a coherent whole. Much discussion was had before anything was recorded about how we would enhance the music with sound effects to help contextualise the period and reflect what was happening on stage in the big scene changes. The music was written specifically to have sound effects placed throughout. It wasn't an afterthought; they were woven into the fabric of the music. This meant that (where necessary) the end of a music cue would blend seamlessly into an establishing sound cue, meaning the audience were never unintentionally 'alienated' by marking it as a moment.

It was especially satisfying to be able sync up detailed sound and music moments with physical movements of the set on stage. From a sound-design perspective, the New York scene change was able to suggest the childhood of a young boy; the traffic, bustle, energy and construction of the rising skyline of the young city; before drawing our focus to a domestic lift rising through floors and arriving in Nina's apartment. The sound designer Chris Shutt balanced these effects with the music and placed them carefully within the structure of the score so that music and sound worlds were as one. This was a particularly useful addition that helped to contextualise the music and tell a clear story.

 **STRANGE INTERLUDE**

Often, if you're setting a scene, you can blend the end of the music with the soundscape of the location. As a crude example: if you're transitioning into an early morning, outdoors, garden-type location, the sound design may feature the sound of birds chirping and perhaps some light breeze rustling in the trees. If the music fades out at the end of the transition, the soundscape can crossfade with it and ease an audience into the scene very gently. Or you could counterpoint the gentle sound design with some contradictory bold music. As well as incorporating these sounds into the music, you can also use them as a thematic idea for the music, writing birdsong into a woodwind part perhaps. Indeed you could do many of these things at once. In any case, you need to understand what the sound design is doing and similarly a good sound designer will want to know what you're thinking musically. In this way you can keep the production feeling seamless. Make the music world and the sound world part of the same thing.

Sometimes you can try to do too much with a piece of music. Remember, an audience will fill in the gaps for you, so you do not necessarily have to include all elements of story, character and location into every scene change. What can be useful is compartmentalising the various action points that occur during the change and using them as a narrative map for the score. In the New York scene change for *Strange Interlude* there were several practical moments from the point of view of the set that would provide signposts along the way: the arrival of the Art Deco staircase, the arrival of young Gordon (who could become a focal point as he ran about the escalating set with a toy aeroplane), the arrival of furniture and finally the arrival of the other characters. The end of the previous scene gave an opportunity to briefly reprise Nina's theme, which could act as the genesis of the music and then expand into a much grander piece to complement the epic nature of the rest of the scene change.

It takes all of the theatrical departments to create an effective scene change, so as well as thinking about how the music will deliver the next scene; you have to make sure it works in sync with lighting, set and technical aspects. These are also continually developing throughout the rehearsal and technical process.

Strange Interlude was unique in that we were able to use computer-generated visual automations to show how the set would move for each scene change. These videos illustrated how all the major pieces of set would move and approximated timings for the completion of each part. This is pretty uncommon, but it made the approach clearer for all departments to understand and gave us an opportunity to more easily storyboard the change in detail before the technical rehearsal. Of course, these timings are only estimates and remain fluid so, as always, I needed to be ready to adapt and edit the music as we went along.

Scoring

Pre-recording

These days most of the scores written for plays are pre-recorded. With the advent of home studios and relatively cheap recording costs in professional studios, most theatre producers will try to avoid the cost constraints of having to employ a band of musicians to play live every performance. Not only is there a huge financial incentive for this to be the case, but from a technical standpoint once the show is up and running, variables are eliminated and the music will sound exactly the same every night. At the time of writing, the biggest mainstream theatre company in the UK that employs live musicians as a matter of course is the Royal Shakespeare Company. The National Theatre still does quite often, but only the RSC does it for every show. There is a section on live music later in this book, but for now let's look at the pre-recorded score.

From a compositional point of view there are, of course, various benefits and drawbacks to pre-recording a score. If appropriate and at all possible (and this usually depends on budget) I like to record some form of live instrumentation as part of any score. With the continual technological advancements of instrument-sampling software, there is a lot you can create that sounds quite authentic entirely from your computer. Using software like Logic or ProTools you can manipulate instrument libraries and synthesizers so they sound (if required) like real instruments or you can create new sounds to suit your purpose. If you're after that 'authentic sound', many instrument libraries now painstakingly record real instruments with a mind-bogglingly thorough choice-combination of timbre, attack, decay, sustain, release and playing technique, whilst also providing different sizes of ensemble and instrument combinations. This is an incredibly useful and powerful resource to have at your fingertips, but I find that for individual instruments (particularly solo strings) there is nothing currently that produces quite the same sound as the real McCoy. Some sounds are getting pretty close though. What many theatre composers do these days is augment live instruments with computer-generated ones. For example, a good way to create a more authentic string-ensemble sound without a full string orchestra at your disposal is to record a live string instrument (commonly a violin or cello) and blend it with sampled strings.

It's worth mentioning that, today, some composers will opt only ever to write with computer-generated samples. On television this can work pretty well. Although home sound systems have grown incredibly advanced, the expectations of a television audience are different to those in a theatre. The nature of how television music is mixed with other sound elements (voice-over, dialogue and soundscape) and then heavily compressed means poor-quality sounds sometimes slip under the radar. In the theatre every sound is amplified several-fold through the huge rig of the sound system. This can expose all manner of bad instrumentation and poor mixing.

Of course, it depends what style of music you're writing, but remember that whatever you do, it's going to be played loud and there's nowhere to hide. Be careful – sometimes orchestral MIDI samples that sound good on small speakers or headphones, don't translate quite as well as you might have hoped.

With a limited budget and resource for recording live instruments, you must make your instrument choices very carefully. This will obviously depend on the style and scale of play you're composing for. I find that normally, with a small-scale play, perhaps something that starts at a regional theatre and goes on tour, producers will not want to pay more than (at time of writing) £800 for the music to be recorded.

We will look at budget breakdowns in more detail in a later chapter, but for now let's assume that that will get you no more than three musicians and three hours in a reasonably priced studio. You must make sure to use that time wisely.

Musicianship

One of the great bonuses of recording live musicians, and the part of the job that still constantly takes me by pleasant surprise is that good musicians take the music you write and make it sound better. Of course, they may be playing every note exactly as written by you, but they add an incredible amount: their individual expression, their phrasing, their years of experience and knowledge of both the instrument and the style of music they're playing, their skill in the recording studio to incorporate slight variations (if necessary) on every take, their participation in receiving and even suggesting notes; in short: their musicianship. For me, a piece of music that is designed to be played live is not complete until someone actually plays it; then and only then does it really exist. One of the other hallmarks of a great musician is their willingness to collaborate: to take what you've written for them and make it the best it can be. A good musician must not only be technically sound, but possess the spirit of the enterprise they've joined. When a musician asks a question about a piece of music, if they have a phrasing suggestion or an idea for a variation, listen to them. These are the people who spend their lives working with their instrument – they will know it better than you do so absorb, consider and, above all else, learn.

Each instrument has its own idiosyncrasies that as a composer you may never learn from a book or a course, but over time you will pick up these little bits of knowledge and apply them to your ever-increasing arsenal. These are small but very useful things – such as where to place trills on a clarinet so they don't cross over the break, to harp pedalling – that you will pick up with experience, and you'll normally find most players more than willing to share their expertise.

Having real musicians engage with your music widens the circle of collaboration. The more brains with different areas of expertise you have tackling a project, the more interesting solutions are likely to arise. We know that theatre is by nature a collaborative art form, and this can apply to the score as well. As long as you get everyone you're working with on board with your concept (and with instrumentalists that's about providing them with clear, well-written, coherent parts and giving good direction as to what you're after), good musicians will only enhance what is already there in your writing. The first time a good musician reads my music, engages with it, and brings it to life is always a thrilling experience, and this happens every time I write something new. I may have spent hours, days or weeks working on the score on my own, so hearing it played back for the first time I feel like I'm finally arriving at something tangible. It's then I can begin to see what I've created and where I need to take it next.

Case Study: *A Little Hotel on the Side* at the Theatre Royal Bath

When I wrote the music for the farce *A Little Hotel on the Side* by Georges Feydeau for the Theatre Royal Bath, I decided to write French-pastiche accordion-led music. In order for this to sound at all authentic (within the world of this production; it's *my* take on French accordion music) I needed to record a real instrument being played by a competent musician who understood the form. I can honestly say at that point I had never written anything for an accordion that would be played on an actual accordion. That may sound silly, but quite often (at least in theatre scores) if an accordion is only minimally featured in a score the temptation is to settle for a sampled version on a keyboard. In that case you write out a keyboard part and don't worry about accordion notation. Of course when you're writing for a real instrument you have to write it out properly, so be sure to look up how accordion scores are notated and categorically provide the most comprehensive scores you can.

In addition to the accordion, I wanted to feature a Django Reinhardt-esque acoustic guitar and, as the budget allowed it, a small drum-kit for rhythmic interest. It's worth considering that had I only recorded the accordion in isolation, it would be a pretty disconcerting (but not impossible) experience for the player. I really needed to set the melodies in context with some form of harmony, as supplied by the guitar. It was a bonus to be able to record live drums on this score – they helped to keep the feel of the resulting music live, even though we recorded to a metronome.

As previously mentioned, the best thing to do on a tight budget is to record the instruments you really need to hear live (drums was a luxury), and then add more sampled instruments later. In this case, I knew I wanted to add an upright bass and some bits of piano and percussion. After I returned from the studio, I was able to do this by syncing up the recorded tracks on Logic and recording MIDI bass and keyboards over the top.

 **A LITTLE HOTEL ON THE SIDE**

Period Instrumentation

When considering the function of your score and how you'll achieve the desired sound, you may come across the proposition of using what are termed 'period instruments': that is, instruments not found in the modern orchestra or featured in a typical modern soundscape. Most instruments have evolved into the things they are today. Ancient descendants of the string family range from the vielle to the rebec to the lira da braccio (all precursors to the violin). Many of these instruments are still in use, and can be utilised to create a unique or 'period' sound. Period instruments are commonly used in scores because they possess a quality unfamiliar to the modern ear or because (with a live score) a director wants a certain look. If an instrument has a unique tone or timbre, it can really help transport your audience to a distinct yet unfamiliar world. And helpfully, as music cues in plays tend to be economically short, a unique instrument or sound can help to catapult the audience into a new space very quickly. However, be careful that you don't expect the instrument to do the work for you. It's how you write for the instrument that will make it a success for your production.

It's not always necessary, however, to use an instrument from the period of the play. There may be a temptation to try and make the score sound 'authentic', but it's worthwhile remembering that authenticity is relative to the production you're working on. What's one person's 'authentic' is another person's gauche.

It would be fascinating, for example, to write for a nyckelharpa (a fourteenth-century, stringed Swedish instrument which looks like a cross between a fiddle and a harp), but out of context and if unseen by an audience they might assume that what they're listening to is a violin or viola. Some instruments, although subtly unique-sounding in isolation, may pass by completely unnoticed by the modern ear especially when only a part of a larger ensemble. The music or instrument geeks amongst us may find it fascinating, but remember that in a play, the music is only serving the production. Also, when dealing with a live score, you don't want an audience being too distracted by what you consider to be a remarkable instrument choice. However, this is not a sole reason not to jump right in and use a nyckelharpa (and I applaud you if you do), but from a practical point of view, you're also going to have to find someone who can play it.

Case Study: *Berenice* at the Donmar Warehouse

When I scored Alan Hollinghurst's translation of Racine's Roman-set French tragedy *Berenice*, I spent a long time listening to film scores of movies set in ancient Rome and to modern recordings recreating what we assume to be the music of the period. There was, universally, much use of wind instruments. Some sounded like flutes whilst others were clearly something more unique.

I became obsessed with the sound of the duduk, which is an ancient double-reeded instrument from Armenia. So I dived in, writing lots of very filmic music which was to feature a duduk and human voices creating something that I thought would be at home in any Hollywood blockbuster. I found singers and a duduk player who were ready to overdub the demo to make it sound authentic. You can listen to an example of one of those early demos, in which the duduk didn't even make the cut.

▶ **BERENICE a**

However, when I played the demos in the rehearsal room, something just didn't fit. It's difficult to explain sometimes why a music cue doesn't work, but I convinced myself for some time that this would still be the right direction to go in. The trouble was that at that point I knew that what I had wasn't quite right, but I didn't have any better ideas. This was a classic case of the composer hoping that he would get to write a Hollywood blockbuster-style score, when in reality it wasn't what was called for. It wasn't until the last week of rehearsals, two days before I was due to record the live portion of the music, that the director hit the nail on the head. This wasn't an epic piece of theatre (although as a tragedy it was pretty epic in emotional scope); it was a chamber piece. Once I understood that, I quickly got that this score didn't need to set geographical place or time; it should be an emotion-led score. The music had to encapsulate the drama inherent between the characters in the story rather than the setting of the scene. I (rather quickly) wrote a whole new score for string trio using the chamber works of Bach and Handel as inspiration. The result was a much more intimate and engaging score. It didn't say 'ancient Rome' at all – and yet it totally fitted with the aesthetic of the production.

 **BERENICE b**

Uncommon Instrumentation

In Stratford-upon-Avon there is a building buried within a street full of car showrooms and garages, slightly off the well-worn track of tourists and Shakespearean scholars. There is nothing in the area that would suggest that you were in beautiful antiquated Stratford. From the outside, it looks like some long-forgotten warehouse, and yet it is home to one of the most extensive, diverse and eccentric collections of musical instruments in the world. This is the RSC instrument store. And it is magnificent.

My first job at the Royal Shakespeare Company was writing the score for Mark Ravenhill's version of Voltaire's *Candide*. It was an exceptionally tonally diverse production and the music spanned a huge range of styles. I was taken to the instrument store by the music department's 'instrument keeper' and allowed to rummage around and take whatever instruments I thought might be useful for the production. Because the RSC stages so many plays (in particular, historical plays) with live music, composers in the past have acquired a huge range of weird and wonderful instruments. Mostly these instruments end up in the storeroom, and many of them would be completely unknown to anyone except an obscure instrument expert. After a happy half-hour rummaging through this treasure trove, I came away with a trunk-load of instruments most of which I never looked at again. However, there was every chance I'd find myself in a scenario where an instrument might unlock the inspiration needed for a unique musical moment in the play.

At the end of the day, your job as a composer is to enhance the story and fit your music seamlessly within the production 'world'. Weird and wonderful sounds and timbres can help keep your score unique if they're appropriate. But remember that in the theatre, nothing is real, so be creative and choose instruments judiciously.

Case Study: *Coriolanus* at the Donmar Warehouse

When I scored the Donmar Warehouse's production of *Coriolanus*, the brief was to create a hybrid-world of ancient and modern. The action was still set in ancient Rome, which made sense of the battle scenes and the famous sword-duel, but the design, particularly the costume design, evoked a much more contemporary feel. With Josie Rourke, the director, it was decided that the music should continue along this contemporary line and perhaps go further.

One line in the text particularly stood out for me as a useful hook on which to base the score. It was this description of the lead character, Caius Martius: 'he moves like an engine, and the ground shrinks before his treading'. Even though the use of the word 'engine' wouldn't have had quite the same meaning at the time the play was written, we felt there to be such a charged atmosphere when this character (played by Tom Hiddleston) was on stage, that when he clashed with others (including the famous sword-duel with Aufidius, played here by Hadley Fraser) there was a palpable sense of 'the machine', 'the mechanical' and electricity about it all. The entire play felt dangerous, like a live wire sparking in a rainstorm. It was because of these statically charged performances and our partially modern design concept that we decided to make the sound world reverberate in an electronic and distorted way. Never before on a play have I collaborated so fully with a sound designer than I did with Emma Laxton here.

Most of the music was written in the rehearsal room and composed on a laptop. As I was writing 'electronica' music, I was able to immerse a lot of the sound design completely within the musical score, and Emma could do the same vice versa. For instance, she would share a sound effect of a static charge being released and I would pass it through filters, play with it, reverse it, compress or distort it and turn it into a part of the music. I could also give her tones – high-pitched string lines or low rumbling drones – which she would sample, distort and build into the sound design of a scene. This was a particularly fruitful collaboration to the point where it was difficult sometimes to discern what was 'sound design' and what was 'music'. When collaborations are as successful as this one, the work isn't necessarily easy but it's incredibly rewarding. You feel very secure because you have someone you trust implicitly enhancing your work, who is on the same wavelength as you are. As a composer you'll spend so much time working on your own it's vital to maintain and treasure these very special relationships and nurture them for the future.

 **CORIOLANUS a**

Case Study: *Man and Superman* at the National Theatre

George Bernard Shaw's *Man and Superman* is a lengthy and challenging play of operatic scope that takes as its source the Don Juan story. There are specific references in the piece to Mozart's *Don Giovanni*, and the epic nature of Simon Godwin's National Theatre production made it clear that the music would have to evoke Mozart's sense of scale and drive.

It occurred to me that if I was going to achieve something that embraced the theatricality of Mozart's score I wouldn't be able to do it with a small number of musicians. Budgets being what they are, I decided to attempt something I'd never done before and combine recorded orchestral samples of Mozart's score with new music. This way I could use small phrases from the orchestra as building blocks to reshape moments from the original score into something new and (more importantly) useful for telling the story of this production. I could then augment them with new writing.

I wasn't interested in moments of singing from the opera, only instrumental phrases. I tried to carry thematic context from one story to the other where possible, but part of the joy of the experiment was to take snippets from different arias and combine them to create something new. From a practical perspective I also needed moments that fitted together in terms of tempo and key. A lot of the music I ended up using was from introductions or endings of arias, occasional instrumental breaks or even moments between sung phrases.

The process of preparing all of these building blocks was lengthened greatly by the fact that no one ever recorded *Don Giovanni* to a metronome, meaning the tempos of the recordings ebb and flow a lot. I had to do an awful lot of time stretching and compressing to get all the music to sit on the same tempo grid.

After this process, what I ended up with was essentially a musical toolbox, or palette, comprised of tiny moments of *Don Giovanni.* I could then start the process of 're-composing' by putting these samples together in new ways and writing new music to glue the whole thing together. We recorded a small ensemble of instruments (string quartet, French horn and clarinet) that had to tune to the pitch of the original recording. This inevitably provided a few moments of consternation due to the peculiarities of European orchestras tuning to slightly different frequencies, but it worked out pretty well in the end.

The final result was an orchestral score that used Mozart's themes in an original way to tell a different story.

 **MAN AND SUPERMAN**

Finding the Form

Timings

After you've marked out all the potential moments for music in a play, it's a good idea to try and get a sense of how long any major scene changes may need to be. At this early stage in the rehearsal process it's impossible to get exact timings but most directors (and designers) will have an ideal. Moving pieces of set, quick changes or furniture turnover mean scene changes inevitably run differently once you get into the theatre. As with the National Theatre's production of *Strange Interlude*, it's a good idea to have a storyboard of what needs to occur to get different pieces of set on and off-stage. Most of the time in the rehearsal room it will be the assistant stage manager (ASM) who changes small dummy bits of set around and places new props, often assisted by the stage manager or deputy stage manager. Whilst timings of scene changes from the rehearsal room can never be relied on to be accurate, what you are able to get a sense of (and from information the designer and director can provide) is what needs to occur between scenes from a technical standpoint. From this you can imagine an ideal timing for each scene change. Also use this as an opportunity to get a sense of any narrative that is carried through the scene change that you can incorporate into your score.

Once you've worked out the approximate length that each cue needs to be, you can start to think about how much music there is space for, and how expansive you can make each cue and the overall musical journey. It's worth saying that directors tend to want scene changes to be as brief as possible. You can do lots of clever musical things between scenes with your score, but ultimately the play needs to flow as naturally as possible. This usually manifests itself in directors ruthlessly cutting unnecessary extra seconds from scene changes. Prepare to be told to cut a fifteen-second piece of music down to ten, and then to seven. If you're ready for this then you may be able to keep a semblance of your thematic through-line no matter how brief the cues become.

Opening Music

If your play begins with a piece of opening music, whether it's an overture or simply curtain-up music, you need to work out how you want the audience to respond. You have to take into account the settling of an audience at the top of a show. As house lights fade, people take their seats, conversations get quickly wrapped up (commonly not as quickly as we'd like), sweets get unwrapped, mobile phones get turned off (hopefully), jackets get removed and people generally need a moment to settle down. If the play opens with a line of dialogue, you want it to be delivered to a captivated and attentive audience. You need to take all of this into consideration when working out your timings.

A very experienced lighting designer once told me that normally he budgets twelve seconds for house lights to fade at the top of an act to allow an audience to settle. It makes sense that an audience tends to begin to focus once the house lights have dimmed completely and they are in darkness, but they commonly don't completely quieten down until the curtain rises and the stage lights are on. Taking all of this into consideration, you have to work out how you are going to grab their attention, but also how you transition them into that first scene. You want the music to lead the audience, so they all arrive in the world of the play and the first scene together.

Scale and Scope

We have already mentioned the budgetary constraints of composition in typical theatrical productions, but this should not be the ultimate dictator of the music you write. If you want to create a big sound (and the play warrants it) then you need to work out a way to do that in spite of any financial restrictions. As well as budgeting the appropriate amount of money to record your music, you must also be aware how you measure the score in relation to the amount of space there is for music in the play. If your opening sequence is relatively short, for instance, you must make sure you don't try to do too much in too short a space of time. Perhaps you want your audience to be stirred up by a piece of music, or startled or unsettled, but if you try to cram too many ideas into a short sequence your score will feel overblown. This applies not only to the scale of your piece – how many instruments and how big a sound, but also to the scope – how thematically complex a piece is and how it's designed to develop. Therefore, make sure you ration your ideas and themes. With a play (or indeed any evening in the theatre) you want each music cue to exist as a part of the whole. Each piece of a jigsaw may be beautifully painted, but only when every piece is assembled in the correct formation can you see the picture. Obviously, inherent in a show's transient nature is the notion that it is always moving. If a play, by its spirit, has captured an audience then they will leave with an impression of the whole. Don't try to do too much too quickly.

Thematic Mapping

When you have worked out where music is needed in your production and what function it serves, it's always a good idea to sketch out how your themes might develop. Sometimes you may attribute a theme to a character or a location, or you may want to trace an emotional arc through a piece. Maybe you want to build tension as the narrative ramps up. In every case it's likely that you will want the score to evolve. It can help to write down the list of music cues and the ideas behind them: the characters, locations, story events and emotional context behind each. Then look for patterns or links between them. Think of reasons why you might want to tie certain themes together and how they might relate to the story arc. From this you can start to assemble a musical map of where and how themes recur. Make sure that you don't see this as set in stone, however. Be ready to adapt as things change through the rehearsal process.

Sometimes a cue by its function will seem to exist outside the palette of the rest of your show. That can be okay. However, you will want to find a way to tie it in even with the most tangential reasoning. Even though a cue may exist as an entity on its own and not necessarily contribute to your overall thematic development, it will still be a part of the patchwork of the evening. Unless you have a good reason for it, it's not a good idea to have something that's so far outside the world you've set up for the rest of your score that it consciously registers with an audience and pulls them out of the story. There will always be exceptions to any rule, but it's worth reminding yourself that it's not always good to be noticed. As a side note it's also worth remembering that, more than anyone else involved with the production (or even seeing it), you will be the person who notices and cares about the reasoning behind musical choices. For me it's a matter of pride in a good job well done. Often, very detailed and thought-through work goes unnoticed, but that is the nature of scoring for theatre. Sometimes it's even the hallmark of a good score. In certain circumstances, if people don't notice the music but are affected by it then you're doing a good job. Composing music for the theatre can provide you with ultimate satisfaction if you're doing the full job to the best of your abilities. Don't cut corners.

Case Study: *Privacy* at the Donmar Warehouse

James Graham's play *Privacy* at the Donmar Warehouse concerned rights issues surrounding privacy in the digital age, particularly in our usage of the internet. It was so up to date with current news stories and technological advancements that the script changed almost on a daily basis all the way through rehearsals. This necessitated the 'score map' to remain mostly fluid right up to the last weekend before technical rehearsals.

The play was also incredibly eclectic in style and delivery and the music had to reflect this. There were stand-alone moments that if looked at in isolation wouldn't feel particularly connected to other parts of the score, but this was a show about something as varied as the internet, so the opportunities for diversity in musical style were huge. It ranged from a sketch about how to take the perfect 'selfie' (which had an underscore similar to a reality television show or infomercial) to a jingle (sung live) about 'Article 8' of the human rights convention, to a meditative underscoring of a reading from Shakespeare's *The Tempest*. Although these moments might have felt musically completely unconnected there was also a more linear score that was planted throughout the evening helping to support the dramatic narrative. This score helped to connect the disparate musical elements, allowing them to become metaphorical 'stops' along the 'road map' of the musical journey. At the end of the show there was a moment where dialogue from the world of the sketches and the narrative musical theme connected. This created a curious release. The final recapitulation of the linear theme set against what had been an earlier 'fun moment' of dialogue seemed to fuse the disparate elements, but set them in a new, more foreboding context. In a way, it was possible to complete the musical journey without resolving it.

I wanted all the music to sound somehow warm but with an element of the 'computer-generated' about it. This was, therefore, an ideal moment to use computer-generated instrument software. Even though many computer samples are now so good that they sound real, there was something that seemed contextually right about generating everything digitally even if an audience wouldn't clock the difference.

 **PRIVACY a & PRIVACY b**

Keys

As well as tracking how your themes develop throughout the play, make sure to keep an eye on how cues relate to each other in respect to their musical keys. The most basic advice is to keep keys varied. If you're developing a theme that recurs throughout an evening, you're likely to develop it melodically and harmonically. That can be enough to push forward a story, but an extra bump up or down in key signature can also help add tension if necessary. Bear in mind, however, that your cues may modulate inside themselves, so it may be the resulting key that you want to relate to your next cue. Even if there are long scenes between music cues, it can help to keep the music fresh to vary each cue's tonal centre. Every scenario will be different so there are no set rules, but if you have a theme that keeps coming back in the same key it can start to feel a bit stale.

Varying keys is also most useful when dealing with bows or 'curtain call' music. I come across this a lot with comedies. If you're using music for the curtain call, it's always a good idea to set it in a different key to the final cue of the show proper. This will be a case in which one music cue follows on from another without a scene in between, meaning the change of key needs to be noticeable enough to make the curtain call feel fresh and slightly unconnected to the show proper. I sometimes find it quite effective to modulate down for the bows, perhaps by a major third from the last cue, but with the melody set an octave higher. Of course every scenario will be different, so experiment with different options. If you're using bows music it's also an opportunity to rattle through your musical themes (if appropriate) in all manner of keys. To be honest, if like me you want to show off, you can normally do it in the curtain-call music.

Sometimes, no matter how much you plan in advance and how accurate you think your timings are going to be, you can come a cropper in the technical rehearsal with a scene change that takes much longer than anyone anticipated. It's always a good idea to record various versions of every cue, but occasionally you may find that you have to start chopping and pasting cues together to make something work that is long enough.

Case Study: *Relatively Speaking* at the Theatre Royal Bath

When I composed the score for Alan Ayckbourn's *Relatively Speaking* I decided to record violin and acoustic guitar in a Gypsy-jazz style inspired by Stéphane Grappelli and Django Reinhardt. In my recording session I covered (I thought) all bases in terms of cue length and necessary feel, but in the technical rehearsal I realised I had nothing that could cover an unexpectedly long scene change. I had recorded many cues in different keys, which also constantly changed key mid-cue, so combining them was a little trickier than if they been constant in their key signatures throughout. The trick was to find a piece of music that finished in the appropriate way to lead into the next scene, but also to find something that started in the best way to finish the previous one. Unfortunately, cobbling these together from the tracks I had recorded resulted in the two pieces of music being in different keys. Without the resource to re-record anything except perhaps to add a MIDI piano note or two I had to find a way to make them sound like they were meant to go together. My solution was to chop the first track mid-flow in a manner that sounded like an intended interrupted cadence and add two MIDI piano notes that acted as leading notes into the next piece of music in the new key. It was definitely unorthodox and would never have crossed my mind to try had necessity not called for it, but it ended up working rather well in the situation. I considered this a happy accident despite the fact it took an inordinate amount of cobbling together.

 **RELATIVELY SPEAKING a**

Storyboarding

Besides the technical necessities of covering the scene changes it's important to understand what purpose the music serves for the experience of the audience. Perhaps it's there to maintain or drive forward dramatic tension from one scene to the next or to underpin a sombre or reflective moment and hold an audience's attention. Quite often it's about maintaining the suspension of disbelief for an audience so that they don't break out of the world of the play when quite obviously non-literal world things are happening. Yes, an audience may never completely forget that they are in a theatre watching a pretend character interact with a pretend set, but they will lose themselves in that world until something external breaks it. There is nothing more likely to break the reality of a pretend theatre world than a stagehand entering the playing space and moving furniture around.

Sometimes, a director will make a clear choice to break the suspension of disbelief by lowering the curtain. In this case an audience is told very clearly that they can disengage. This is particularly common in a comedy as sometimes an audience needs a small breather and the opportunity to check in with each other is welcome. If there is a quick turn-around of set, you can keep the house lights lowered in the auditorium and an audience will happily sit and listen to some music. There is only so long that this can hold, however. No matter how wonderful the music is, an audience has been conditioned to engage both visually and aurally with the show. If they then have nothing to look at for much longer than a minute, you'll find they become restless, the momentum of the evening will be broken and the scene change will look like a mistake. If a change of this nature is much longer than a minute, a director will likely do one of three things: either give the audience something to look at as well as listening to the music, allow them to disengage by turning house lights up a little whilst keeping the music playing (which feels a bit like an advert break on television) or decide to have a formal interval; which will be an ordinary length of fifteen to twenty minutes if it's the main interval in the evening, or can be a mini-interval of five minutes or so. It's important that the choice is made clear to an audience so they don't feel abandoned while you turn your set around.

The Train Journey in Relatively Speaking

In our production of *Relatively Speaking* there was a major scene change between a London apartment and a country house and garden, which we always knew would take at least two minutes. This was unavoidable but too long to go unmarked. We had to come up with something to cover it. It was too early in the evening for an interval (the first scene was only twenty minutes long) and it also felt too early to go into a holding state of half house-light.

At the end of the first scene of the play, one character chases another across the countryside in a train. They both arrive at a country house at different times and a comedy of mistaken identity ensues. The set and costume designer, Peter McKintosh, designed the front cloth as a map of the countryside on which we could trace the journey of the train. Small lights were woven into the cloth along the train route that lit up so we could track the characters' progress. This seemed like a good idea to keep the audience engaged with the world of the show, and by adding in some lively Gypsy-jazz music with some train sound effects to enhance the chaos of the chase, seemed likely to be enough to cover what was an epic scene change.

Of course, the first time we got into the theatre and tried it out, the change took about four minutes, which is (clearly) far too long. With rehearsal it got much quicker, but even at just two minutes, interest in our map and my music began to wane. I had anticipated this when originally writing the score, so had incorporated other 'interests' into the music. I'd built in several 'stops and starts' to suggest stations and unexpected delays, and also moments where we slowed the pace down very quickly to suggest that the train was slowing or breaking down. Interesting as I thought this was, once we were in the theatre it became clear that these 'features' weren't quite enough on their own. Something else needed to happen sonically, so we decided to add countryside sound effects alongside the train ones to enhance the detail in our 'journey' and make it a much more literal and narrative moment. There was even an opportunity for someone to have 'switched to the wrong train' which meant the lights went off on a tangent across the map and then had to about turn. Even though all these elements felt individually small, when combined they added up to a pleasurable narrative journey.

The lesson I learned here was that if you can continue the story of the play when scenes have stopped (for necessary technical reasons) then an audience will follow, trust that the production knows what it's doing and be entertained enough to remain engaged. In this instance, once the scene change became technically efficient and the music and soundscape much tighter and clearer in terms of its storytelling, by the time the curtain rose to reveal an entire house and garden onstage, the whole sequence felt very much like a *coup de théâtre* and the audience applauded.

 **RELATIVELY SPEAKING b**

It's also worth noting here that set designers often say that if you do a scene change behind a curtain that lasts longer than a minute, an audience will expect something significant to have changed. If for instance, the curtain rises and the only thing that's different is that some cutlery has been set, you'll be in trouble.

Case Study: *Noises Off* at the Old Vic

Sometimes a half-house-lit scene change with a curtain can come as a bit of a relief to an audience. In our production of *Noises Off* by Michael Frayn there were three major scene changes, but only one interval. After Act One we had an interval as normal, but between Acts Two and Three we flew in a front cloth and played some 'holding music' in half house-light. There had been similar music playing pre-show, as the audience were coming in, so we used the second mini-interval as a chance to continue this, making it clear to an audience to stay put. Audiences were laughing so much at the end of the second act that they welcomed the opportunity to compose themselves, breathe and interact with each other before the final act commenced. Therefore there was no incredible rush or requirement to try and sustain the suspension of disbelief, and there was no confusion as to what this moment was: setting the house lights at half and playing the holding music made it clear to an audience that the show was neither over nor breaking for long. Brilliantly, Frayn also wrote the beginning of the third scene as happening in front of the curtain, so even though the audience were able to have a breather, they were never in fact out of the world of the play.

Transitioning Between Scenes and Music

How you introduce scene-change music at the end of a scene will obviously vary depending on the scene itself, but there are a few common scenarios that we can look at here. Sometimes it's a good idea to creep in some introductory tones under the end of the scene as a way of gradually transitioning from the scene into the music proper. This is particularly effective if there are further stage directions after the last line of dialogue. Alternatively, you might want the music to make a hard entry, especially if there is a snap blackout. Whatever you do musically, it's likely that the lighting designer will want to echo that with lighting (or vice versa).

Case Study: *The Winslow Boy* at the Old Vic

In our Old Vic production of *The Winslow Boy* by Terence Rattigan, at the end of the first act Arthur Winslow makes a phone call followed by the stage direction:

> *He replaces the receiver and then, after a moment's meditation, turns and walks briskly into the dining room. Curtain.*

As previously mentioned, my score for this production was ragtime-flavoured using only clarinet and piano. The next scene in the play occurs nine months later so I wanted the music to convey a sense of time passing. The mood at the end of the scene was pensive and sombre so I elected to underscore Arthur's last movement with solo clarinet. A single note on a clarinet can be such an expressive thing in its simplicity: because it is so pure and sparse, an audience fills in the required emotion for you. It can be mixed so that it almost appears subliminally at a low level and crescendos into perception.

The storyboard of this transition was that the clarinet tone would arrive just after Arthur replaces the receiver so that it registers in the '*moment's meditation*'. When Arthur breaks away it was a good cue to transition to the full music. This was the plan, but an even better solution arose when we got into the theatre and saw the set. As Arthur walked towards the dining room, he had to slide open the upstage dining-room doors to enter. This revealed the family inside who looked up expectantly. The sliding doors provided a solid physical hook to tie in with an ascending melodic flourish that led into the new piece of music. This allowed us to maintain the solo clarinet tone for longer than we had anticipated, gaining us a more gradual but ultimately wider crescendo. This longer build helped to create more tension before the release of the music and the subsequent flying in of the curtain.

 **THE WINSLOW BOY**

Pushing the Narrative Forwards

Quite often with plays, the thrust of the music is most usefully geared towards the scene that it is establishing, not the scene that has just happened. This is normally because the goal is to keep the story moving forwards and to keep the changes as brief as possible. It's important that the play doesn't 'stop' just because a scene has ended. Composers spend most of their time in the theatre trying to make sure scene changes feel a part of the play as a whole and are not equivalent to advert breaks in television. Sometimes, however, as in the previous example with the clarinet tone in

The Winslow Boy, in order to introduce a new feel with music you need to transition first from the establishing scene. The snappiest scene changes are the ones where the music begins boldly by grabbing the narrative and driving it forwards.

Case Study: *Coriolanus* at the Donmar Warehouse

For the Donmar's production of *Coriolanus*, my electronica-flavoured score often arrived unapologetically at the end of scenes. Perhaps it was the nature of this play (and certainly this production), where the stakes were so incredibly high and the characters so passionate and driven, that enabled me to make the score bold and direct on its entrances. Good actors will be sensitive towards this drive and to the needs of the production as a whole. Often the strong delivery of a final line in a scene can really help to catapult the show forwards.

There were also a great number of scene changes and transitions, so it was necessary to introduce them in a concise manner. We used many subtly planted tones and underscores, but these tended to run under scenes to enhance the storytelling rather than as a way to creep in an introduction to scene changes.

Case Study: *Much Ado About Nothing* in the West End

In Josie Rourke's West End production of *Much Ado About Nothing*, I wrote a 1980s pop-music-themed score using many of Shakespeare's lyrics from across the canon and setting them as if they were hits from the '80s. This was an especially fun score to write and due to the star power of Catherine Tate and David Tennant, the production was sold out before we began rehearsals. This meant that I had a rather healthy budget to record the music, so I was able to spend a week in a recording studio creating an entire album's worth of '80s-inspired Shakespeare songs and instrumental music. One of the key elements of the first half of the play was a disco party scene where music needed to run constantly in the background. I was able to combine the music for the change with the introduction to a song that would then play in the background of the new scene. The music travelled (courtesy of the sound designer) from the main house speakers (for the scene change) and back into the PA of the onstage DJ's kit. In this way it went from being non-diegetic scene-change music to diegetic background party music.

The music was very much mixed into the background in the scenes so the dialogue was clear, but in between exchanges or scenes it could be turned up and used to punctuate a scene change. As we moved into the latter stages of the party, the music slowed down and created that 'end of the party slow dance' feel. Without this background music, the overall dynamic of the scene would have been drastically different.

 **MUCH ADO ABOUT NOTHING**

Buttoning

How to transition out of a scene change into an establishing scene also throws up a few options. One of the most direct methods of ending a piece of music is by using a button – an accent at the end which is precise, clean and bold. They are often used in comedy in conjunction with a lighting snap to start a new scene with a lively and comedic feel, or when a scene starts mid-conversation. If a production uses a curtain and the characters are already onstage, one of the easiest ways to join a scene mid-conversation is by raising the curtain (with music) in blackout, snapping the lights up and buttoning the music once it's complete. Buttons are also useful for the end of scenes for comic effect to heighten a laugh or lead applause.

Fading

Another option for completing a music cue that transitions into a scene is by creating a fade that either runs under the first line of dialogue or fades out as the lighting state completes. It's possible that it may be some time before any dialogue begins in a scene, so you can encourage an audience to focus in on the world of the play by creating a subtle fade out (often cross-faded with some ambient sound effects). Sometimes music can continue under a scene. In this case, it's good to consider how it relates to the scene as it progresses. Make sure the music sits beneath the scene and not the other way round, unless in special circumstances. The transition music will now have become underscore – we will cover this more later.

Case Study: *Men Should Weep* at the National Theatre

The opening sequence for *Men Should Weep by* Ena Lamont Stewart at the National Theatre, directed by Josie Rourke, had almost a filmic sensibility. The brief for the music was 'Gershwin does Glasgow'. Set in a tenement block in deprived 1930s Glasgow, the set the audience saw as they entered was the front of a tenement block the height and width of the Lyttelton stage.

The music had to give a sense of the era, and of the spirit of the people who lived in the bleakest parts of it at that time. Jazz music seemed to counterbalance the inherent poverty with an energy that was defiant, youthful and vibrant. As the house lights went down, the first part of the music cue was intended to suggest, in a manner reminiscent of Gershwin, the skyline of Glasgow. I considered the sound world of this moment to feel almost like an establishing shot in a movie. At this point the music comprised of a solo clarinet and muted trumpet, mixed in with sound effects of dockyards and city noises. This helped to introduce this 'other world' and kick-start the audience's imagination. We built on this with a crescendo leading into an energetic drumming pattern, which led all the windows in the tenement block to be flung open and the women of the tenement started shouting out to their various children. Suddenly the world had become populated and alive. This was a good way of emphasising the energy of this place, these people and the chaos of life in this particular neighbourhood.

Once the final window was slammed shut, the entire wall split in two horizontally and moved apart to reveal the cross-section of three floors of the tenement building. This was a pretty awe-inspiring sight and the music and sound had to support it. As the walls split apart loud sound effects of rumbling and breaking could be heard, stylised in a way that made them non-literal. We weren't trying to say the walls were actually splitting apart, but it was a wonderful way of drawing an audience even further into the world of the play. As the walls shifted, the music grew in intensity as more jazz solos bled on top of one another. This helped to emphasise the chaotic interior of this building and the energy of kids who ran up and down the stairs revealing small glimpses of family life inside each of the apartments. As the lights began to focus in on the central room (which was the only one fully visible and the setting for much of the play) the music went through another change: a lot of the jazz faded away and distilled down to a single clarinet, marking out the individuality of this house against the jazz-fuelled noise and chaos of all the others. In a film, the camera might have moved through the outside wall or window and into the room. In our version it was a way to pull the audience into our world, to make them feel like they'd arrived in and engaged with the setting in which the drama was about to unfold.

I find film analogies particularly useful in looking at big sequences like this. Here were three stages of transition in the opening sequence from a musical and sound point of view. It opened with what we could term the sonic 'aerial shot', which set the scene of 1930s Glasgow. This then linked to the sonic 'establishing shot': where we focused on the tenement, illustrating the energy and liveliness of that neighbourhood. Then we moved to an 'interior shot' which pulled us right into the room where the first scene takes place. The whole sequence felt like a journey, even though it took place in under two minutes. By the time the dying strains of the last clarinet note faded away, the audience had hopefully completely suspended their disbelief and were now immersed in the world of one room.

It's worth noting that from a practical point of view, no matter how well a piece of music achieves the setting of a tone or location, sometimes you have to acquiesce to practicalities. In the original version of the music for this opening, I had quite a full-sounding jazz ensemble playing under the dialogue of the women shouting from the tenement windows. It was very quickly clear that without mic'ing the actors, you couldn't hear them over the music. The solution was to strip down this part of the cue to just drums and bass, which meant we could keep the energy, drive and rhythm of the music but could also hear the dialogue over the top. It was a fine balance in terms of the mix between the recorded sound and the live voices of the actors. Had the music been much quieter, we would have lost the drive and impetus we'd built and the bottom could have fallen out of the sequence. The upshot was that it meant the transition following it, where the wall split and moved, could be built from a much quieter place enabling us to exploit a much wider dynamic range. The more interesting a sonic journey is for an audience, the more involved they will feel when they reach the first scene.

 **MEN SHOULD WEEP**

Case Study: *The Physicists* at the Donmar Warehouse

The opening cue for *The Physicists* by Friedrich Dürrenmatt was also an exercise in transporting an audience to a new world. Set in a Swiss sanatorium in the 1960s and featuring a lot of ominous violin music offstage, the play opens at the scene of a murder. I had written pre-show piano music, which I could only describe as 'muzak', or 'elevator music'. This was music designed to sound completely innocuous on the surface, but underneath something about its repetitious and soulless nature hopefully led to a swirling sense of madness. It was very tonally safe. It didn't swerve towards anything that might be interesting or emotionally affecting, but if an audience member had been sat in the auditorium from the time the house opened, hopefully by the time the play started, the music had made them feel anything but relaxed.

Following this, the opening music cue continued this piano theme but swiftly became more chromatically interesting as the lights began to fade. With a sudden crescendo and a blinding swell of light, this music gave way to a screaming violin solo and total blackout. Collaborating with the rest of the creative team was vital so that lighting, music and sound could overwhelm an audience into a place of total uneasiness. The Donmar has a thrust stage so there was no curtain to rise. From a practical point of view, unless we wanted the murder scene on stage for the entire pre-show, the cast would have to assemble during this opening cue. Once the audience were overcome with the incredibly bright light in this moment, the darkness of the blackout that followed was pretty much all encompassing, enabling the cast to assemble for the murder scene without being easily noticed by an audience who were mere feet away. This is an example of how you can physically alter sense and perception and use them to your advantage.

 **THE PHYSICISTS**

Extending this idea, one of the most entertaining and affecting openings of the second half of a play I've composed for was also for *The Physicists.* I took the piercingly loud, screaming violin theme from the opening sequence and transposed it to a new key, but this time there was no introduction or warning. When the call was given for the second half of the play to start, the entire auditorium was plunged into a sudden blackout as incredibly loud and abrasive violin music was played. This was, I thought in my glee, the closest thing to a roller-coaster I've created in a theatre. Previously I have mentioned the power you can assert over an audience with sound. This was one moment where an audience couldn't help but be startled and hopefully were put on edge for the first scene in the second act of the play.

Underscore

Underscore is typically defined as background music that helps to indicate and enhance the mood of a scene.

It can be subliminal in the way that an audience doesn't consciously register it, it can be more prominent in setting the mood, or it can be a feature of a scene that morphs between diegetic and non-diegetic worlds. Sometimes underscore can work in opposition to the action on stage, thereby contextualising it in an unusual or subversive way. There are marked differences between the way underscore functions in film and in the theatre. In a film, the dialogue can be mixed to ride above the music, meaning you can control exactly what your audience hears no matter where in the cinema they're sat. In the theatre, actors tend not to be mic'd most of the time, which means the level of music that can be played under them has to be limited. Also, an audience in the theatre are spread out across sometimes several levels so the sound coming from one un-mic'd actor will vary depending on your proximity to the stage. Theatres are built to be acoustically helpful to un-mic'd performers, but the nature of the live medium means their dialogue is not controllable in the same way as it is on film.

The level of concentration and necessary participation for an audience in the theatre is greater than in the cinema. A theatre audience must tune in and focus. Being in the same room as the actor and hearing their voice acoustically is one of the thrills of live theatre, but it does mean that underscore in theatre productions has to be cleverly thought out. The acoustics of each individual space have to be taken into consideration. Sound designers will ensure that the entire audience has a similar level of audio coverage from the sound system, but they can't (without mic'ing) control an actor's voice in that way. And nor should they. I once heard a famous theatre and film actor talk about a performance he gave (that was mic'd). One night he decided to give a speech with a bit more 'welly' than he had before and couldn't understand why his voice wasn't punching through the auditorium. Afterwards, he spoke to the sound operator who told him he'd turned the volume level down on his microphone because he was 'louder than usual'. This negated the actor's control over his 'live' performance and he refused to wear a microphone on stage again. This is another reason you have to be very careful about underscore in the theatre – actors can, and will, give different performances every night. I've heard actors say this is part of what attracts them to the theatre – the ability to improve and modify a performance throughout a run.

There are two ways in which this can affect your underscore. The first is the changeability of the sound level of the performance and the other is in the actual nature of the scene. Resident directors will help actors to keep performances steady throughout a run, but the live nature of the medium means that it will inevitably change as they experiment with new ways to approach lines. As a composer you have no way of knowing how the performance will change over time, so you have to aim at and write for the performance that happens on press night. However, if you write something too prescriptive that sits under a scene it can limit the actor's ability to 'play' and may render the evening a little flat. I've also had actors tell me that they do not like the audience being told 'how to feel' by underscore in their scenes. Fair enough. It is an actor's job to tell a story. Music can really help with that – but if they don't respond well to it, you may find you have an uphill battle to reach a point where everyone is happy. It's worth noting as well that as a composer it's necessary that you have a grasp of the production as a whole. It's very difficult for actors to look at a show they're in from an outside perspective. It may be that underscore perfectly supports an actor's performance in a scene, but if they do not respond well to it, it will be the director's job to either encourage them to work with it or look for another solution. Bear in mind that actors have to turn up every night and give the performance. They are the ones who will have to deal with the music on a long-term basis. Try to see it from all perspectives.

Another difference between film and theatre audiences is in the level of suspension of disbelief that must occur. Cinema is an all-encompassing medium that propels the viewer into a world that is projected forty foot high. A regular cinemagoer doesn't need to work too hard to enjoy the latest blockbuster. The experience is brought to them. Theatre audiences need to participate actively in the imaginative myth-making of an evening. More is expected of them; they need to bring themselves to the experience. They are required to remain present and engage in an emotional contract with the performers who in turn have to build a new performer/audience relationship every night. Besides tuning out of the reality of the theatre building itself and into the 'live' performance, an audience is asked to imagine the reality of a set which may be somewhat figurative or, in the case of promenade theatre, physically walk from place to place whilst still maintaining a suspension of disbelief (and without falling over). A fully engaged audience can drastically alter a show. Their reactions will change the pace and timings of scenes (especially with a comedy) and contribute immensely to the energy of the evening. Audiences are an enormous and crucial element of what makes any theatrical performance a success.

Typically stage plays use less underscore than films although, when it works, it is to great effect. One of the basic features of underscore music in either film, television or theatre is that the bits directly underneath the dialogue tend to be simpler than the bits in between the lines or scenes. Underscore done badly becomes a distraction and we know that in the spoken theatre the words rank above the music in almost all circumstances. Underscore therefore tends to be melodically quite simple and unobtrusive, but again it varies greatly in its usage.

One of the simplest and most common types of underscore in the theatre is the subliminal drone. This is a single tone or note that lies under a scene, framing it or suggesting a context. Commonly drones are on the lower end of the sound spectrum and give a sense of foreboding. (See the earlier description of infrasound). Drones can utilise both elements of music and sound design. For instance, a combination of a low steady instrument or software sample can blend with a sound effect of a low-end engine noise or hum to create a drone that is unique and unsettling. Every moment will require a different sound or timbre, but drones are frequently otherworldly and disconcerting. Drones can be wonderfully ambiguous and subjective as well. Depending on their context they can ask an audience to interpret meaning and prompt feelings they may personally associate with that sound. Drones can provide instant shifts in mood: they don't tend to move melodically but they can morph sonically into new sounds and build tension in doing so. At a low level, sometimes an audience will be hardly aware of their existence (hence the idea of subliminal), but there may well be occasions when you want the drone to feature in a scene in a very assertive manner.

Case Study: *Coriolanus* at the Donmar Warehouse

In our production of *Coriolanus* at the Donmar, there were lots of drones. Due to the minimalist nature of the set design, we used quite a lot of sound to contextualise location and mood. One particular drone I recall as being very effective was in Act Five, Scene Three, at the entrance of Volumnia, Virgilia and Young Martius. They enter to greet their son, husband, and father, Coriolanus, after a long estrangement. They have come to appeal for mercy for their city and their people. At this point he is a banished warrior, determined to bring his former home to ruin, and completely lost to the comforts of home and family. They have no idea how he is going to react, so there is a huge amount of dramatic tension at this point in the play.

In the text, Coriolanus has a speech detailing their arrival and the conflict between their former affectionate relationship and his ambition to let their city burn. In our production, as they crossed the stage, a subtle change in lighting and a subliminal drone helped not only to create a sense of a new event, but also created a sense of pressure and unease underneath Coriolanus's lines. At this point the drone wasn't only underscoring the text but also the movements of the other characters in the scene as they walked towards him. In a way, the drone pulled us into a moment that existed 'outside time' or at the very least slowed time down.

This wasn't, however, an ominous drone – it continued the sonically electric theme of our production by mixing a high-pitched hum that buzzed and tingled with a very low, almost-inaudible pedal tone. Our original draft for this moment was much louder and sat in a sonic middle range that made us all feel quite nauseous. It helped to contextualise the moment but it was too heavy-handed and left little room for the scene itself. It's possible for a drone to become stifling and claustrophobic, which can be useful in the right circumstance, but there's a difference between building tension and making an audience slightly uneasy, and making them feel sick. Other drones were planted throughout this production, often just lifting a moment or highlighting a movement. When a score is as sonically comprehensive as this, the moments you choose not to score become as important as the ones you do. If a drone has been playing for some time under a scene, the moment you stop it can be very useful to point up the line of dialogue immediately following.

 **CORIOLANUS b**

Case Study: *Candide* for the Royal Shakespeare Company

Besides drones, underscore can be used not only under dialogue but in moments of action. In the RSC production of Mark Ravenhill's *Candide*, the first act was a play within a play staged in an eighteenth-century Venetian countess's palace. The play within the play was meant to evoke an eighteenth-century French operetta in style and was mostly underscored in that fashion. Being a production at the RSC, I had a live band of seven musicians to work with on this particularly ambitious project.

This scene was to be staged partly in a large-scale Pollock's Toy Theatre that integrated various set pieces including a ship at sea, cardboard waves and a huge storm. There were several songs interwoven into the dialogue, but the plan was to underscore most of the act in a style comparable with traditional melodrama (in the eighteenth-century sense of the word, *melodrama* meaning 'music-drama' – the art of combining spoken word with short pieces of accompanying music).

Melodrama

We often associate melodrama with hammy over-acting or moustache-twirling villains, but in fact, melodrama dates back to the stage plays of the eighteenth and nineteenth centuries. The term comes from the French *melodrame* (spoken drama that uses some musical accompaniment), but ultimately from the ancient Greek word *melos*, meaning 'music or melody' and *drame* meaning 'deed or theatrical act'. In this context it is simply defined as drama with incidental music, or an operetta with spoken dialogue; a piece in which speech and song alternate.[23]

Misha Donat wrote an interesting article in the *Guardian* a few years ago mentioning how melodrama excited Mozart:

> 'Nothing has ever surprised me so much,' wrote Mozart enthusiastically to his father after seeing Georg Benda's melodrama *Medea in Mannheim*, towards the end of 1778. 'It is not sung, but only declaimed, and the music is like an obbligato recitative. Occasionally there is also speech underneath the music, which makes a marvellous effect. Do you know what I think? One ought to treat operatic recitative in this way, and only have sung recitative when the words can be well expressed by the music...'
>
> As a self-contained theatrical form, the fragmentary nature of both music and text in the melodrama meant that it had its limitations, but the intervention of an individual melodrama within an opera could be highly effective.
>
> ...the sudden intrusion of the spoken voice into opera has been used by most composers ever since.[24]

In our 'play within a play' retelling of the tragic and wildly adventurous life of Candide, because I was writing music influenced by eighteenth-century operetta and melodrama, I didn't intend it to be subliminal in any way. This was music that was as much a part of the storytelling as the actors were. However, one of the biggest challenges I faced was how to underscore the un-mic'd dialogue so that the actors could still be heard. This music had to be quite adventurous and full, and was thematically complex and boldly melodic and theatrical – a completely different set of rules to a more modern interpretation of a play. We had to balance the mic'd sound of the ensemble (violin, trumpet, cello, double bass, keyboards, percussion) with the voices of the actors in the 'thrust' theatrical space (which is very difficult to do, especially if you don't know the acoustics very well). We were aware of moments when there was action without dialogue so we could use the band in its full force. It turned out, due to budgets, that we were only able to mic four people at a time, so those characters that had songs were allocated the head-mics, and all other dialogue, if it was set over music, would have to be balanced acoustically. This was the first time I'd done this, so it was a learning curve. Essentially, if you're underscoring in an acoustic situation such as this, it helps to write in pitches that are dissimilar to the voice of the actor you're underscoring. If the frequency of a female voice is, for instance, similar to that of certain strings on a violin, it can be difficult to distinguish the voice if the instrument is playing at the same time. It's preferable to underscore a voice with an instrument of a considerably different pitch and timbre.

Had this been a ballet or fully realised opera, the music would have been the core constituent, but because this was in essence an operetta within a play, it still needed to support the world of the spoken actor. It was complex but well worth the time it took to work it out.

Music could help to support the story of what was happening in the character's internal narrative, the external action of the scene or the mood of the story at any point. In essence, I was able to write much more descriptively and 'on the nose' than I could normally for a play. A lot of the time when writing music to underscore drama you're trying not to be noticed. The music should be subliminal or at least only a supportive part of the whole. In this production, the fact that the music was for a 'play within a play' and also in a melodramatic style meant that it could very much stand out as a narrative force in its own right. In this respect it was indeed very much closer to an opera than a play.

At one point in the story, a storm causes the destruction of a ship at sea and in our Pollock's Toy Theatre version, this involved cardboard waves and what could be described in a modern sense as 'theatrically heightened' acting. This part of the play was very much rooted in storytelling in a literal sense, but here was an opportunity for the music to take the reins for a moment and become fully operatic in scope. In this instance, the underscore was able to overpower the actors at the point the wind would naturally have drowned them out and assume control of the narrative. There was nothing naturalistic about this moment – Soutra Gilmour's brilliant design featured a very stylised wooden boat and waves sat within the antiquated world of an eighteenth-century production. Even though every constituent part was heightened and of that world, it didn't make it any less believable. If you thoroughly commit to a concept, an audience will get on board with whatever reality you wish them to accept.

Writing a score in this style gave me a wonderful sense of release and freedom. Even though I was writing in a particular Baroque idiom (which brings up certain specifications and forms to follow), the opportunity to fully embrace the drama and use music to tell the story was particularly rewarding.

Underscore in the spoken theatre is mostly concerned with supporting mood rather than creating narrative. When the opportunity to paint a world with music comes along, it's worth grabbing with both hands.

Catchiness and Identifiability

Sometimes it becomes unhelpful for a scene if your music is very hummable or memorable. As someone who spends a lot of time writing songs, it goes against everything I feel innately, but if an audience becomes too aware of a piece of underscore it may detract from the action on stage. Also, depending on the content of the production, it may be inappropriate for an audience to go home 'humming the tunes'. A lot of the time you can write music that is very memorable and catchy, but firstly it has to serve its function in the piece. If the music is there to set a tone or mood, be careful it doesn't overstate its presence.

Necessary Cuts

When working on an older play (something that is well out of copyright), a director may move things around or make cuts to help give a clearer sense of the story (for that particular production). Most modern audiences are accustomed to shorter and more distilled theatrical experiences than in the past, so revivals often get trimmed down and distilled. In 'Shakespeare's Audience: The Groundlings', Amanda Mabillard describes how the nature of theatre audiences has changed:

> Shakespeare's audience was far more boisterous than are patrons of the theatre today. They were loud and hot-tempered and as interested in the happenings off stage as on. One of Shakespeare's contemporaries noted that 'you will see such heaving and shoving, such itching and shouldering to sit by the women, such care for their garments that they be not trod on... such toying, such smiling, such winking, such manning them home... that it is a right comedy to mark their behaviour' (Stephen Gosson, *The School of Abuse*, 1579). The nasty hecklers and gangs of riffraff would come from seedy parts in and around London like Tower-hill and Limehouse, and Shakespeare made sure to point them out in *Henry VIII*:
>
> > These are the youths that thunder at a playhouse,
> > and fight for bitten apples; that no audience, but

> the Tribulation of Tower-hill, or the Limbs of Limehouse, their dear brothers, are able to endure.[25]

Even with twentieth-century plays, cuts often help to keep an evening skimming along. Our production of Eugene O'Neill's *Strange Interlude* at the National Theatre managed to cut what was originally almost five hours long (with interval and dinner break) to a more succinct three hours twenty with an interval. The director, Simon Godwin, had a theory: 'People [the audience] would have got quite drunk in those two intervals... so in the original there was a lot of repetition, which I think was basically O'Neill going, "We need to recap for people after these long gaps."'[26]

Sometimes when cuts are made, and scenes moved around, moments for new bits of music present themselves.

Pastiche and Parody

Often when considering the function and style of your score, a director will point you in the direction of some music they like or think appropriate to the play. This is common and normally very helpful. Of course, if they just wanted to use a specific piece of music then they wouldn't need to hire a composer, so these suggestions are typically only there for you to reference as part of your research. Remember, no music is created in a vacuum. All music is influenced or inspired by what came before. You may be creating what you think of as a whole new sound, but just by the nature of it 'feeling new' means you are comparing it to something that already exists.

When you are asked to write in a particular style or take influence from another composer's work it helps to be clear about the differences between pastiche and parody.

Webster's Dictionary defines *parody* as 'a literal or musical work in which the style of an author or work is closely imitated for comic effect or in ridicule'.[27] The literary theorist Mikhail Bakhtin thought that parody was a 'natural development in the life cycle of any genre' in that it 'will always reach a stage where it begins to be parodied'.[28]

Webster's defines *pastiche* as 'something (such as a piece of writing, music, etc.) that imitates the style of someone or something else'.[29]

In 'Postmodernism and Consumer Society', the academic Fredric Jameson elaborates:

> Parody capitalises on the uniqueness of... styles and seizes on their idiosyncrasies and eccentricities to produce an imitation which mocks the original. I won't say that the satiric impulse is conscious in all forms of parody. In any case, a good or great parodist has to have some secret sympathy for the original... the general effect of parody is – whether in sympathy or with malice – to cast ridicule on the private nature of these stylistic mannerisms and their excessiveness and eccentricity with respect to the way people normally speak or write. Pastiche is, like parody, the imitation of a peculiar or unique style, the wearing of a stylistic mask, speech in a dead language: but it is a neutral practice of such mimicry, without parody's ulterior motive, without the satirical impulse.[30]

Pastiche has become a dirty word in theatrical circles in recent years, which people often substitute for 'unoriginal', but I don't subscribe to this view. In the theatre, you will always be composing within a framework, or under the influence of the writer or director. This doesn't make it any easier or any less artistically valid. Entire movements such as neo-classicism and neo-romanticism could be considered pastiche. Classical music is strewn with pastiches. Prokofiev wrote his *Symphony No. 1* in loose imitation of Haydn and Mozart, and Edvard Grieg's *Holberg Suite* is a pastiche of eighteenth-century dance forms. In pop culture, Michael Jackson's 'Thriller' takes its style from horror and zombie movies from the 1950s to 1980s, the television show *Family Guy* can be seen as a pastiche of traditional American family sitcoms, the *Indiana Jones* films are romantic pastiches based on 1930s adventure serials, and much of Quentin Tarantino's work is also very openly pastiche. By its very nature, pastiche is what helps to make all these so entertaining.[31]

Any music you write for the theatre will be unique in that it is written specifically for the purposes of a particular production. You can write pastiche or hint at any number of styles, but though the music has the flavour of something familiar, it will structurally be something particular and therefore new.

Music Up-close

When examining forms of music and specific eras with a view to referencing their style, it helps to deconstruct and look at the music on the most fundamental level. This may feel like it's sucking out all the joy and mystique of the piece, but when you once again listen to it reconstructed, hopefully you will find that not only does it still hold together, but that you can now spot new levels of intricacy and detail which make the listening experience even more enjoyable and fascinating.

I once attended a sound-technology lecture on deconstructing the production behind a piece of pop music. The lecturer told us that by the end of the lesson we would all be unable to listen to or enjoy music in the same way again. I found this to be untrue. Even after all this time, and after studying and deconstructing many scores, I can still get completely lost in a great piece of music (or indeed a great piece of theatre or cinema). I am still able to switch off the analytical part of my brain and be carried away on a journey (when it's good). I consider this to be an asset. It also means I can get completely absorbed in the process of creating art, which is one of the best reasons for doing it in the first place.

If, for just a moment, you set aside the intangible artistry of a piece, temporarily ignore all social context or function and look at each note and chord individually, you will become aware that writing music, when everything else is stripped away, is fundamentally about making choices. Is it this note or that note? This chord or that? This modulation or another? Although these choices will be influenced by a whole plethora of things, not least context and function, different styles of music tend to have a set of distinctive forms and characteristics. Outside of artistry, these fundamental elements are signifiers that distinguish one style of music from another. It's far from an exact science, but when you examine music in this way, you can start to see the patterns that occur in different music types. It can be a useful tool to make yourself a checklist of the principal things you think make up the distinguishing features in a specific type of music. These could be anything including typical instrumental forces, common chord progressions, melodic phrasing, harmony choice and form. This doesn't feel terribly satisfying as it negates the 'magic of the whole', but it's a good way to force yourself to zoom in on a musical style in order to understand its chemical make-up.

Form and Content

The musicologist Richard Middleton suggests that there are 'two poles around which, traditionally, discussions of works of art revolve. *Form* is supposed to cover the shape or structure of the work; *content* its substance, meaning, ideas or expressive effects.'[32]

The overall plan or structure of a piece of music on a macro level is known as its form, but form can also be used on a micro level to describe how the individual frames or beats of a piece of music hold together to create a phrase. Thus even through-composed music has a form which can be analysed. The nineteenth-century music critic Eduard Hanslick said, 'Music is forms put into motion through sounds.'[33]

In the western world, most people will be able to recognise macro form in a straightforward pop song (i.e. the difference between a verse and chorus), but may struggle to identify more complex forms exploited in larger classical works or in unfamiliar types of music from different cultures.[34] However, the crowd at a rock concert doesn't become entranced because of the form of the music – the direct magic comes from its content and the context in which it's being performed. In-depth analysis of the 'content' of music is a monumental task unsuited to the remit of this book, but we can get a grasp on how to understand the form of a piece of music which can affect or inform its content.

Middleton suggests how we could see form in terms of the process of composition:

> Andrew Chester, Charles Keil, and some other writers have made a distinction between musical categories... on one side, it is suggested, is music which is produced by starting with small components – rhythmic or melodic motifs, perhaps – and then 'developing' these through techniques of modification and combination to end up with a unique, extended, sectionally articulated or through-composed structure. On the other side is music which starts with a framework – a chord sequence, a melodic outline, a rhythmic pattern – and then extends itself by repeating the framework with perpetually varied inflections to the details filling it in.[35]

These theorists see the distinction being made clear through comparing, in the case of the former, 'the large-scale instrumental music of the European classical tradition (Beethoven symphonies, for instance)' with the latter's 'open-ended African and Afro-diasporic variation forms (jazz improvisations on a pre-existing tune or chord sequence, the lengthy percussion pieces of many West African cultures)'. They see that 'historically, popular music in the USA and Europe seems to move (although with many variants and diversions) from an approach nearer to the first category to one closer to the second'. But that 'probably no popular music has ever been completely structurally individualistic in the Beethovenian sense'.[36] There are also a great number of modern film and television scores that approach compositional structure as from the second camp, where once they may have sat much closer to traditional classical music.

There are many music textbooks that will explain musical form in great and mind-numbing detail. For the purposes of this book, I'll take a look at how to compartmentalise a form when you come to it. It's not entirely necessary to remember all the various classical forms off by heart, but for the sake of thoroughness I'll include a quick summary.

It's best to listen to a piece of music in its entirety before you start breaking it down. If first you get a grasp of the journey of the whole composition, it'll be easier to then get a better sense of how individual sections (roads, if you will) or moments relate to it. Middleton suggests that 'form depends on statement and restatement, unity and variety, and contrast and connection'.[37]

When breaking down a piece of music into sections, uppercase letters are traditionally attributed to label different sections within a piece and lowercase letters can be used to label different phrases within a section. Each major part of the music is labelled with a letter, starting with A. If following sections of music are exactly the same they are also labelled A. If a section is almost exactly the same but has some marked differences it can be labelled A^1 (pronounced 'A prime'). That section can show up later exactly the same and be labelled A^1 and if a further variation occurs it can be labelled A^2 ('A double prime'). Sections that are clearly different to the A section will be called B and then C, etc. All of these can have prime variations and are labelled in the same way.

Here are some general (and most familiar) forms split up into their sections:

Strophic: A A A, etc.

Binary: A B A B

Ternary: A B A

Typical Pop Song: A B A^1 B C B^1 (D) (Verse, Chorus, Second verse, Chorus, Bridge, Altered chorus, (Coda))

Rondo: A B A C A, or A B A C A D A

Arch: A B C B A

Medley or Chain Form: A B C D, etc. or A A B B C C D D, etc.

Theme and Variations: A A^1 A^2 A^3, etc.

Sonata Form: Exposition: (Theme group 1/Theme group 2) – Development – Recapitulation: (Theme Group 1/Theme Group 2)

Sonata Rondo: A B A – C – A B A

Cyclical Form: Takes its form from the libretto and narrative (originally from opera). Also can be a song cycle.

When examining form and structure, it does help to look at the social context and function of a piece; i.e. if it is a dance there may be set rules about how long phrases need to be, how the piece needs to be structured and what tempo it needs to be played at.

For the sake of this section I'll use a piece of music I wrote for *The Recruiting Officer* at the Donmar Warehouse. In our pre-show section we featured a live band of musicians playing a series of country dances to set the tone for the evening. In this instance, I could easily have used music from the period but decided it would be quicker, easier and more beneficial to write my own. This is because when you're the composer of a piece you have complete control over it structurally and tonally from the get-go. It can take a lot of searching to find an existing piece of music that suits your purpose exactly and, in any case, if it's being played live (as in this instance) you will have to arrange it (or at the very least, write it out) for your ensemble. For this show, I decided to take as my inspiration English folk music such as was featured in *The Dancing Master* (referenced in an earlier chapter).

Folk music is a good example to look at here because it tends to follow quite recognisable patterns in structure. In seventeenth- and eighteenth-century English folk music, typically for a dance, a common structure is often written as AABB. (Which basically means, the first section (A) is played twice, followed by the second section (B) twice.) Typically, it will then loop back around to A to repeat again.

Phrase Structure

Each section of music is divided into a series of (for the sake of easy description: melodic) phrases. Phrases vary in length but tend to be allied to the length of a breath or single bow movement. Phrases exist in relationship to each other by repetition, contrast or variation. If a phrase comes in a pair, it is usually the case that the first phrase feels 'unfinished' (called the antecedent phrase) and the second phrase completes or resolves it (the consequent phrase).

Melodic Phrasing

If we look at a piece called 'Portsmouth' from *The Dancing Master*, we can see how the first section of music (A) is split into both antecedent and consequent phrases.

We can also notice that these phrases can be split up into a further two sections or units called motives. According to Wallace Berry in *Form and Music*, this is the 'smallest characteristic unit, distinctive in melodic and rhythmic content, whose significance is established in development... a stimulus to its own development and continuation'.[38] From the upbeat (or anacrusis) to bar 1 through to bar 2 can be deemed one motive – let's call this (a), bars 3 and 4 are a second motive (b). The third is an exact repetition of (a) and then the fourth is a variation on (b) so let's call this (b[1]) which resolves to the tonic (or home note).

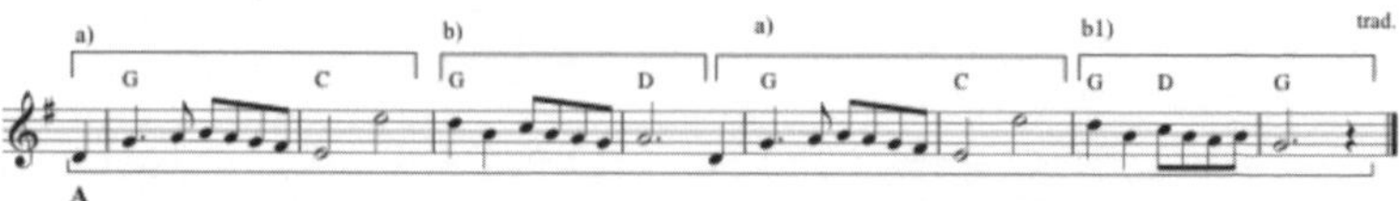

The motive (a) establishes the tonal centre by firmly planting the tonic (or key note) on beat one after a pick-up note (or anacrusis). In this case, from notes 'd' to 'g' in G major. It ends on the unresolved submediant (or sixth degree) of the scale 'e'. This propels the melody into a new section (b) in order to resolve this tension. After resolving that tension, section (b) sets its own by landing on the supertonic (or second note) 'a' with an implied harmony of the dominant chord 'D'. This in turn requires the stability of the tonic chord for resolution, which is exactly what happens next with the return of the (a) section. Once again the (a) section requires a subsequent phrase to resolve the tension of the 'e' submediant, but this version: (b[1]) resolves neatly to the tonic.

This is a simple (apart from all the fancy language) way to examine the tension and release that exists in a melody, both of which are vital to make it exciting and interesting but yet seem inevitable.

This is a typical form for a folk tune to follow. Melodically it provides a sense of complete balance and familiar predictability for the listener. Tension and release are primary proponents of music structure. If each four-bar phrase was a chapter in a novel, it would be impossible to put down: there is essentially a cliff-hanger at the end of each chapter. This helps the ear understand and tune into the very clear structure that is necessary for a social dance. The participants may be unfamiliar with this specific piece of music, but will understand its form by its clarity, simplicity and similarity to other more familiar dance structures.

When emulating this feel, it makes sense to embrace a similar structure. Here is a piece I wrote for *The Recruiting Officer* transposed to the same key and using an even simpler chord structure, following a similar pattern of tension and release.

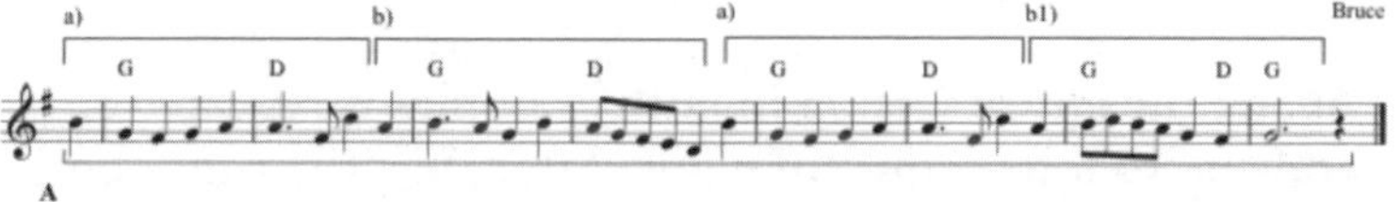

In both of these pieces, this entire section is repeated, not because it is technically unresolved – by the end of the eighth bar, both are harmonically and melodically resolved to the tonic – but because the human ear is conditioned to expect it to. If you consider that dances tend to be counted in eights, then at the end of one section you will have counted two lots of eight. It is then repeated because eight-beat phrases in these types of dances tend to be counted in lots of four.

We then move on to the B section of the tune. In the 'Portsmouth' example we notice that again it can be split up into four units or motives. Melodically, phrase (c) is a variation on (a) but up an octave and with a slightly different ending and (d) is closely related to (b). (It could almost be called (b^2) from a melodic perspective.) The last two phrases are exact repeats of phrases (a) and (b^1) from the A section. The one thing that strikes true here is economy with melody. From this example it's clear that it doesn't require much variation at all to create a second section to a tune.

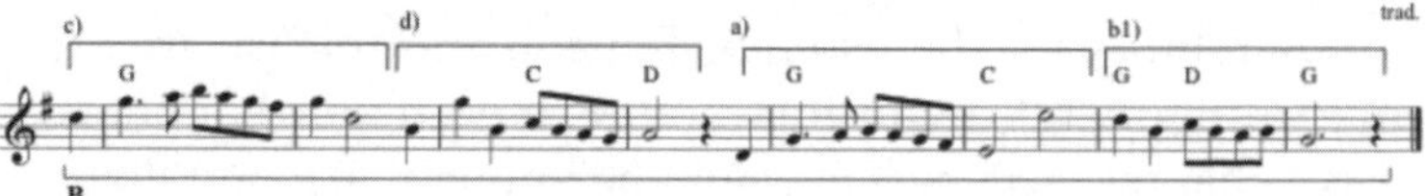

If we now look at *The Recruiting Officer* music you'll notice that the phrases are similarly related to their counterparts in the A section. Rhythmically phrase (c) is very similar to (a), and (d) is rhythmically related to (b). This time, however, the next phrase is a repeat of (c) – which in itself in strongly related to (a) – but again, the last phrase is almost identical to the last phrase in the first section (b^1).

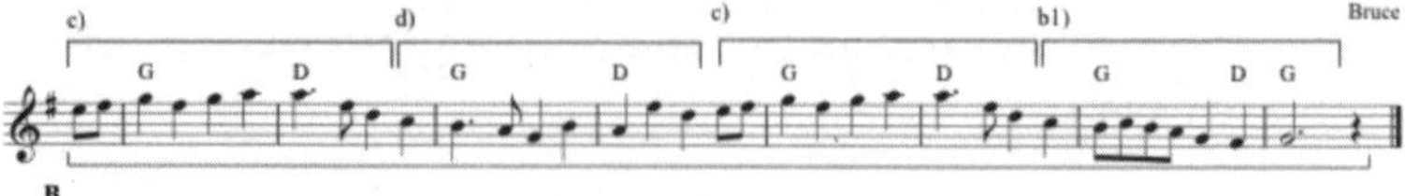

Again, the entire section in both examples is repeated so it adds up to four counts of eight. After this, the tunes both repeat in their entirety several times over. Although they may offer slight variations, melodic embellishments, addition of extra instruments, etc., neither one strays from this structure architecturally, melodically or harmonically.

Harmonic Structure

The harmonic structure of these examples is very straightforward, using only two or three of most common chords in the major scale. These are the chords of the tonic (I), subdominant (IV) and dominant (V) in these cases G, C and D major. Each of these examples ends an antecedent phrase with a subdominant or dominant chord (which to the ear sounds unresolved) and then heads towards a resolving final chord of the tonic to complete the consequent phrase. However simple this may seem, these chords are the basic building blocks of a huge amount of music. A large majority of country, blues and early rock-and-roll songs use three-chord structures. Although most music is infinitely more complex than this, these very common building blocks are frequently at the root, and are, in any case, a good place to start.

This example is a simplified way of looking at how the tension and release in a melody and harmony structure is formed. If you are trying to emulate a particular style, this is a key component to examine.

As a composer you will probably create melodies like this without paying any conscious attention to how they are structured on a micro level. On a macro level you will notice how many bars are included in each phrase and how they are repeated to form the road map of the whole piece. By no means should you resolutely tie yourself to this structure (on either level), but understanding how it works and what 'the templates' are is a good place to jump off from and write something new. In this instance, I wasn't looking to progress the form or stray into new areas – I needed a piece of music to sound like folk music of the period, so employing a similar structure to an authentic piece was helpful.

From jigs to reels to waltzes to sarabandes and so on, most of the music from this period fits into familiar structures all of which were easy for dancers to follow. I didn't have to reinvent the wheel for this purpose – but I wanted to have some fun playing with it a bit.

To readdress the point that I may as well have just used existing tunes (as they would now be public domain anyway). Inside the twenty minutes' worth of music in the pre-show sequence I had introduced most of the melodic themes that were about to be used for the show proper. This was a great opportunity to plant themes in an audience's subconscious at an early stage (akin to an overture) so that when they return later, a relationship has already been formed. Then it's possible to subvert the sense of joy perpetuated in the pre-show by setting the familiar tunes against a conflicting backdrop. If you then develop and recapitulate these themes at a point much deeper into the story, an audience feels like they've come on a much bigger journey.

Often you may not have a score to study to inspire you, so you will have to absorb structures and influences from just listening to a piece of music. Most music will be much more complex than the 'lead sheet' from the previous example so there will be plenty for you to consider, but often melody and harmony structures can be broken down into a similar notion of tension and release.

Imitation, Repetition, Innovation

As mentioned before, all the great composers were influenced by their peers and those who preceded them. Studying scores is an invaluable way to learn, but a word of warning: you can't really distil great artists down to a couple of tricks and habits. Part of what makes some composers sound unique is that they blend frameworks together or experiment with and bend a set series of rules or structures. It might feel like heresy to try and mimic something Mozart or Beethoven did, but this is the way they all learned from each other. Through imitation, repetition and innovation, new pathways can be formed.

Once you've assembled knowledge on overall structure, harmonic and melodic phrasing, instrumentation and cultural references for a style of music, make sure you've absorbed lots of it in whatever guise is available and you'll have a good 'mood board' to assimilate from. If you then think of these ingredients as a lens through which you can refract your own music, you should be able to assemble something that sounds like it came from the world you're examining, but with a fresh and individual perspective. To push abstract analogy even further: if you squashed up all the music references you have side to side into a metaphorical quadrilateral, rotated the whole thing ninety degrees and took a diagonal cross-section through it, this slice of musical and technical ingredients would form the foundations for a toolkit to build a new compositional idea influenced by a particular style.

Using Technology

Using Music Software

These days, technology has advanced so far and become so cheap that almost anyone can get themselves a basic professional standard studio set-up in their home. Most contemporary composers have at least a rudimentary understanding of how to write out scores using a computer program or mix tracks using software such as Logic or ProTools.

Notation Software

Musicians are accustomed to professionally presented scores in recording sessions, and it has become relatively easy to produce them without the need for a copyist. That's not to say that copyists are extinct by any means – many composers still write with pen and paper and give it to a copyist to write out in full or use them to edit or format their scores, but as budgets tend to be quite tight on plays, the more you can achieve yourself, the better off you'll be in the long run.

I grew up in a time when music software (basic though it was) was already available and I began using it as a teenager when writing out scores and creating my own pop songs. That doesn't mean I don't sketch out things on paper first, but the more comfortable I've become with the software, the more likely I am now to write onto the computer directly. I'll normally make some short-hand notes on paper first and then pretty quickly transfer it onto the computer and arrange it there. Music notation software like Sibelius or Finale makes this process quick and relatively painless. The benefits of notation software are numerous for the professional composer: you can write scores quickly and lay them out in a professional manner, you can edit scores instantly without having to rub out or rewrite whole passages, you can playback those scores and hear a MIDI version of them (which makes it much easier if you tend to work a lot by ear), you can see all the staves on your score at once and pull off individual parts for musicians to play, you can also print, email, export scores as MIDI and create audio files making it much easier to share your work. New additions (at time of writing) include the ability for the program to transcribe audio or scan sheet music. This technology will only become slicker and more useful for the modern composer, so it's well worth investing the time and money in it as soon as you can. It will make your job easier and your results will look professional even when deadlines are tight.

There is also the function that enables you to record MIDI and let the program transcribe it for you. In my experience, however, the software is so accurate that it transcribes what I've played exactly to the millisecond. Although it's adjustable for margin of human error or feel, I've found I tend to end up with a score that is over-accurate and therefore messy, and I have to spend a significant amount of time editing it. As I've become more attuned to the specific program I use, I can write a score out note for note much more quickly than having to go through and edit a MIDI recording. In this instance I know I have complete control over every part of it, from the notes themselves, the values and pitches, to the voicing, stave layout and accidentals. I've found that if I write it out properly myself I'm aware of the reasoning behind every note and every marking of expression or technique, just as I would be if I wrote it in pencil. I believe this is the best way to be in charge of your music from the start. Until your score is in the hands of a musician, you are still in total control of it. I believe it's best to know you've thought through every single compositional choice you've made and kept your margins of error to a minimum.

Music software like this is also helpful for playing demos of cues to directors before you record the real versions. Although the MIDI sounds can be pretty basic (they are always improving, and you can spend time adjusting them if you wish), it is still a helpful guide for an imaginative director to get a grasp of the score before you record. This saves you a lot of time and money and also allows you a small sense of security, as you're able to receive confirmation from the director as to whether or not you're on the right track at an early stage.

When using scoring software there are shortcuts you'll learn which will make the process much quicker (as we're always on a deadline). If you're relatively new to writing for specific (perhaps transposing) instruments, programs allow you to write your score out in concert pitch and do the transposition later (when you come either to look at those parts individually or print them off). The program will also keep an eye on the instrument ranges for you, but it's best to learn these details for yourself, as these things are a bit more fluid than a computer program will have you believe. Don't allow yourself to become too reliant on software. As a composer you should use the software as a tool to cut down on time and present professional-looking scores; it is not a substitute for learning about instrumentation or arranging. These are important elements of writing music, whatever method you use. Of course, sometimes you'll be inspired by the software, from what it allows you to do quickly or at least from experimentation during the process of writing with it; but don't allow yourself to become complacent, sloppy or lazy. These scoring programs are a means to an end. Get the music off the laptop and onto the music stands of real musicians if you want to learn what works and what doesn't.

Having said that, scoring software does allow you to get the music into the hands of musicians much more easily and workably. Sometimes musicians like to see the music before they turn up for the recording session, so you can email it to them beforehand. Bringing your laptop with you to a recording session or band rehearsal allows you to make quick changes if something needs editing. You can write out whole new cues in a technical rehearsal with a live band, print them off and run them up to the musicians in real time. That's one of the great achievements of modern music technology – the speed at which music can be written and shared. If keys need to be changed, they can be in a matter of seconds. Even instrumentation can be changed. For example, you may have written quite a tricky part for a Bb trumpet and the instrumentalist would rather play it on one tuned in A. Another advantage of using software is that it is very straightforward to keep a record of all your drafts so you can refer to them later. It also makes it much quicker to produce variations on cues so you do not have to write the whole cue out each time you want to change one bar, and makes it easier to reuse certain sections of music.

There is even the possibility to bypass the process of printing out music altogether. As we can now share music digitally, it is possible for musicians to play from a tablet or screen showing a PDF of the score. This saves paper, printing time and means new edits or versions can be passed on wirelessly. With the addition of a foot pedal that controls the PDF score, you don't even have to take your hands off the instrument to turn pages. As technology evolves, I'm sure there will be even more advantages and time-saving measures built into notation software, but no matter how far the technology advances, fundamentally music is still written by composers. There is no substitute for learning the craft of composition and arrangement. Music software cannot write your music for you.

Digital Audio Workstations and MIDI Sequencer Software

Modern advancements in technology have allowed the 'bedroom musician' to record his own professional-quality tracks and share them with the world. This was one of the great revolutions of the digital age and a remarkable innovation for the amateur musician or composer. The downside was that many of the smaller professional recording studios went out of business. People who could get their hands on relatively cheap software and recording equipment didn't feel the need to pay for the 'professional touch' any more.

This also meant that in the theatre world, composers could produce scores on a much tighter budget. Recording studio costs could sometimes be completely avoided (although musicians will always need to be paid). Depending on the style of music, some scores are now completely created on a laptop with no need to record 'real' instruments at all. If budgets are particularly tight, you may find yourself having to do this anyway, which is far from ideal if the style of music you're writing requires a live or real instrument sound.

In my opinion, professional studios are still indispensable for the quality they produce, and totally necessary if you're recording something with more than one or two instruments. Physical space becomes an issue with the home studio as well as noise reduction. If you have a big enough budget to get your own home-studio set-up and it's large enough for your needs then you may be able to bypass the professional studio on lots of projects.

Professional studios do still, however, have other advantages. Having a professional engineer recording your music with the appropriate microphones, in the appropriate acoustic environment and giving his attention to the quality of the sound and the performances is both another ear that is well worth having in the room and another opinion. Personally, I don't have the same level of recording knowledge as a professional sound engineer so I will always welcome their input when it comes to recording technique and advice. Some composers come from a background in sound technology so are able to do a lot of this work on their own. Bear in mind, however, that as a composer you will spend a lot of time writing music solo. Sometimes the recording studio is the first proper opportunity to let other people hear it and feed back opinions. Another pair of ears can be an invaluable asset. Also, recording in a professional studio focuses the project into the time slot available. The energy of the session will be focused, the participation of all parties assured and the amalgamation of a range of talents directed towards making your music the best it can be. (I will cover the actual process of working in a recording studio later.)

At the time of writing, the two software programs that have become most prevalent in the UK in both recording studios and home set-ups are Logic Pro and ProTools. Both achieve similar results with different interfaces. Logic Pro is described as a digital audio workstation and MIDI sequencer software application and ProTools as an audio production platform (but it is very well equipped to handle MIDI as well). Some recording studios can run both but have a preference for one over the other. If you happen to be working with the same software at home when you prepare your tracks for the studio session, then you can share files directly with the studio which will save you time individually transferring the files from one program to another.

As previously mentioned, it is quite common to record a large part of a theatre score using MIDI instruments and then incorporate real instruments to enhance the authentic sound. Depending on your score and instrumentation, either can come first.

When you record live instruments in a studio, most of the time it is wise to record to a click track (metronome). This keeps tempos regular from take to take. Precision like this makes it much easier to cut and paste between takes and align everything on your screen when you come to edit later on. Sometimes, however, you will want a track to speed up or slow down in an organic way and whilst you can program a click to do either of these things, if there is a rallentando or ritardando at the end of a cue then I often find it better to turn the click off at this point and record 'wild'. This will mean your individual takes will have slight variations in tempo, but it's usually worth it to preserve that human feel.

If you have an extensive backing track ready to go before the recording session and you're only recording one or two instruments, it can be helpful for musicians to play along to this. In my experience, if you're recording any more than that (a string quartet for example) then a lot of musicians will ask you to turn the MIDI instrumentation off and just give them the click to play to. Players in string quartets use each other for intonation and tuning, so any extra unnecessary music playing through their headphones can become a distraction. Be aware, however, that you will want the entire track to be in tune, not just isolated sections tuned individually, so at the very least the section leader should be listening to a fuller version of the mix on headphones. You'll have to tackle each situation individually, but musicians will be quick to tell you if they prefer their headphone mix in a particular way.

Another benefit to recording live instruments first is that their performance may lead you to treat your MIDI instrumentation differently. I will always take the performance of an experienced professional instrumentalist over my MIDI sequenced music. MIDI is much easier to change at a later date, and I would rather my live instrumentalists gave their best performances unencumbered by a MIDI guide. As long as the recording is tight to the click, you can be creative with the structure of the music long after the recording session is over.

Hardware

In addition to software, the modern composer has an ever-increasing array of hardware gadgets to assist him in his creation process. Everyone has different methods so these are not all essential, but a basic set-up would consist of a MIDI controller keyboard and a condenser microphone with a phantom powered interface to connect it to the computer. I personally have a full-sized electric piano with MIDI interface, and a smaller 49-key MIDI controller keyboard with pitch bend and modulation wheel that sits on the desk in front of my computer screen. These MIDI controller keyboards come in all shapes and sizes. Some are small and portable, touch sensitive or might have weighted keys like a piano. They don't usually generate their own in-built sounds. They are purely 'controllers' that trigger sounds generated from your sequencer software, and are great for experimenting with sound as they allow you to assign switches to control different MIDI functions. They currently come with lots of extra functions including MIDI pads which can be used to trigger clips in music sequencers, drum pads allowing you to create beats, and various faders, knobs and wheels, all of which can be synced up to software, velocity-sensitive trigger pads and assignable sliders.

What you require in this aspect will depend on both the style of music you're creating and your process of writing. Bear in mind that composing for the theatre throws up an enormous variety of music styles, so it's good to get your head around some of the hardware that's available to you (even if you're not particularly tech-savvy). A lot of these extra faders and pads are designed for use in a live situation by DJs and live bands to trigger samples. If you are working at home it may be that you don't require all of these options but I'd suggest it's worth embracing the technology. You never know when it might come in useful to generate some new ideas.

Electric pianos do not tend to have the same amount of MIDI controller options but are much closer to conventional pianos in their size and key-weighting. I use my electric piano to record piano parts and use the MIDI controller for individual instrument parts or MIDI experimentation. With time and experience you'll learn what your favourite set-up is. Many composers have built up entire studios full of external audio processors, reverb units and gadgets. Fundamentally, though, you do not need all of these extras to create music. Most of what you require (in terms of home recording) can be found in the programs themselves (and, of course, in you). External hardware just sometimes makes the process more interactive, intuitive, experimental or simply 'playful'.

Plug-ins and Processors

Some of the largest and most useful parts of these software programs are the effects processors and plug-ins. These enable you to edit sounds in an almost limitless variety of ways. This is where you can add or edit compression, reverb, distortion, delay, EQ, chorus, echo, panning, etc. The list goes on forever and gets updated almost daily as new plug-ins are released.

The great blessing with all of this technology is that it opens up a world of possibilities that were previously unavailable to the composer on a budget. Besides the ability to make music using huge swathes of instrumentation you would never be able to afford in reality, the tremendously large scope of electronic sounds now available is pretty mind-boggling. Even better than this, you have the capacity to change and edit these sounds for your own purpose. The most unique or original sounds come from your own treatment of those which come as standard. Using effects processors and plug-ins, the capacity to experiment with and create new sounds is endless. In addition, treating standard MIDI samples of live instruments with modern advancements in compression, reverb and EQ can make them sound even more authentic.

Virtual Instrument Libraries

Virtual instrument libraries are also sounding more and more realistic with every new release. A lot of them are now created by painstakingly recording real instruments note by note, detailing various techniques, velocities, attacks, dynamics, speeds, expressions and so on. Add these to libraries created by leading experimental electronic artists and DJs, and the palette you'll have for composition is pretty exciting. Remember, depending on your working relationship with the sound designer on your production, you may be given some sound effects to incorporate into your score during the composing stage. Without becoming a sound designer yourself you can still edit and alter these sounds to fit in with the rest of your music or use them as instrument sample patches themselves.

Video

Another feature of professional-level music software is that it allows you to import video and synchronise your music to it so you can score to picture with precision. It also allows you to keep track of and easily reference any exact time-code moments the video editor may be using. ('A time code', also known as a SMPTE code, is an electronic signal used to identify a precise time reference across different media to help with synchronisation between different systems.)

In the theatre, video projection is being used more and more, and the ability to compose and synchronise music precisely to fit a video is important, especially when time is of the essence. Now if you want a note of music to happen on a specific visual cue on screen you can make it happen with ease. This means you can be even more creative in the way the music and video interact.

Trailers

Increasingly, theatre producers are creating video trailers to advertise their productions. In addition to the score you write for a show, you may be asked to score the trailer. Often the trailer director will simply ask you for a copy of every music cue from the show and a film editor will choose, edit and cut the music to picture, but sometimes you will be asked to write a new score entirely. It's likely that this will be related to the music in the show but needs to be tailored specifically to fit the trailer. In my experience (and bear in mind that these elements of the modern theatrical process are evolving all the time) theatrical trailers come in four types.

- The first is the montage-type trailer which consists of actual shots from the show that have been filmed live at either the dress rehearsal or discreetly at a preview performance. Sometimes these will also feature audience testimonials.
- The second type is a conceptual trailer, which tells a story independent of the show itself, but based around the show's themes and sometimes style.
- The third type (slightly less common) consists of interviews with experts about the piece, the author or the theatre company itself.
- The fourth type shows rehearsal or backstage footage of the process of bringing the show to the stage.

  (Sometimes, some combination of these is possible.)

The montage-type trailer is the most common and the most likely to use music that already exists in the show. These give a prospective audience little snapshots of the production and lets them know what to expect. Critics of this type of trailer suggest that theatre needs to be seen live and trailers are unfair representations of how the show will feel in the theatre itself. The reality is that people are becoming more and more accustomed to having theatrical trailers to help them decide which shows they'd like to see. It's no different to a film trailer, except that theatre tickets tend to be much more expensive than cinema tickets, so you can hardly blame an audience for wanting a little more information about a performance before they shell out their hard-earned cash. Besides, a theatre show needs to be more than the sum of its parts (and especially the tiny parts you get to see in a trailer) so if an audience is disappointed in the show it won't be because of the trailer. The music is normally either cut from cues you have provided for the video editor or will be live audio from the video footage. The latter is most common in musicals.

The conceptual trailer is becoming more and more popular. Due to advancements in camera technology and video-editing software and the fact that these are becoming much more affordable, small video companies are being commissioned by the larger theatre companies to come up with variations on this type of trailer. Quite often they will feature actors from the show, and sometimes they will use text from the play, but what sets these apart from the montage-type trailer is that they don't attempt to recreate the production itself. They stand alone, akin to cinematic short films or television adverts. The best of these displays a clear concept that has a relationship with the themes of the show, but is not the show. They are as variable in content as the shows they publicise. Critics of this type of trailer say that they are not representative of the show at all and in a way they are right. Yes, an audience is not seeing what the actual stage production looks like, but then that's not a new concept. Before trailers, audiences had to trust in either the company producing the play, the director or actors engaged, the author, the play itself, or they needed to be captivated by the ideas put forth in the advertising material. If the ideas put forth in a trailer excite an audience's imagination then that is as good a reason to buy a ticket for the show as knowing (for example) exactly what the set will look like. This type of trailer is likely to warrant a new score. Normally these are produced before or during the rehearsal period, whereas the montage-type trailers are shot once the production is staged.

Case Study: Supporting Bad Concepts

I was once working on a big show at a major theatre company when I was asked to score a conceptual trailer that fell terribly flat. In my opinion, the problem was a lack of concept. The trailer director had simply assembled a few of the leading actors to pose in front of a green screen that was then replaced with various backdrops. Then they overdubbed some lines from the play. When I was sent the first edit of the video to write the music, it seemed obvious that it wasn't very strong. Part of the problem besides the lack of concept was that it was shot in the first week of rehearsal when the actors didn't really know each other, were still getting to grips with the concept of the production and hadn't done any proper line-work. The result was that everyone looked a little uncomfortable and the resulting trailer lacked any clarity. It certainly didn't sell the show or provide enough intrigue for a viewer to want to pursue it any further. Thus, it was very difficult to write music to. When it was complete no one responded well to it and it was promptly replaced with a montage trailer as soon as they could film the full production. In this scenario I flagged my concerns privately with the director as soon as I could, but still wrote the music as asked. You have to be careful where and how you voice your opinions, but I think it's important to raise concerns if you have them, they're relevant and you're able to do so in a constructive manner.

The trouble is, a bad trailer can give completely the wrong impression of a good show whereas a good trailer can do the opposite. In reality, a trailer is only part of an advertising strategy, but it is rapidly becoming the norm rather than a novelty and you want to get it right.

The third type of trailer, which consists of interviews with interested parties or experts in the play, or the playwright, is often the least related to the concept of the individual production. These types of trailer are relatively uncommon, but they can give an insight into the rationale of the play without giving away any specific production secrets or details. Music for these trailers tends to be unconnected with the show itself as is the aesthetic of the edit and camera work. They tend to be treated more like documentary shorts.

The fourth type, featuring rehearsal or backstage footage, can use a mix of all of the various musical styles we have seen so far. Commonly if they show a rehearsal room excerpt with music or song they will use the audio from that shot, but they can also function like documentaries with their own score. They sometimes consist of interviews with featured members of the company, backstage crew or creative team. These often give an insight into specific production details like music or costume. Audiences enjoy seeing the backstage process of how a show is put on, so this type of trailer can be quite popular. Sometimes a combination of backstage and actual footage (from the montage-type trailer) gets you the best of both worlds.

Writing Songs

Songs in plays perform a variety of functions. Sometimes playwrights incorporate them directly into their plays by writing their own lyrics; sometimes they specify existing songs and either quote the appropriate verses or leave it up to the discretion of the individual production to choose the right bits; now and then they will suggest a song be written to fill a moment and give a guideline to what they're after; occasionally a director will ask for a new song to be added to a scene in a play (this more often happens with plays that are long out of copyright); sometimes a song is used in place of scene-change music; and sometimes a director may ask you to musicalise a part of a scene or a piece of verse that was not intended to be musicalised by the author in the original script.

William Shakespeare wrote a lot of music into his plays, from the poetic lyrics in the comedies to the ceremonial drums and trumpets of the histories and tragedies; there are over one hundred songs alluded to or included in his texts. Only a few of the original settings of Shakespeare's lyrics have survived: the best known being Robert Johnson's version of 'Where the Bee Sucks' and 'Full Fathom Five' from *The Tempest*. Although there is no conclusive evidence these were used in the first or early performances of the play, there's a pretty good chance these are the originals.[39]

Shakespeare's England was a very musical place. As H.B. Lathrop in 'Shakespeare's Dramatic Use of Songs' attests, singing was incredibly popular:

> Singing was universal in England in Elizabethan times. It is also, of course, well known that the standard of vocal accomplishment in those days was not high. We have authentic records of the much later introduction into England of the Italian art of singing. With the advance of the art, singing has become more and more the business of specialists, who sing much better than anybody in Shakespeare's England... there was neither regular concert nor vaudeville in those days, the legitimate theatre was the only place where public singing could be heard; and hence an actor who sang agreeably was listened to with a patience such as no modern audience would show. The abundance of music in Shakespeare's and other Elizabethan plays is nothing individual, but was the most natural thing in the world, when England was still vocal and merry.[40]

Case Study: *Much Ado About Nothing* in the West End

These days most composers write new musical settings of Shakespeare's lyrics for their productions. One of Shakespeare's most famous lyrics, 'Sigh No More' from *Much Ado About Nothing*, has been set hundreds of different ways by various composers, sometimes even for purposes outside the context of the play. In Josie Rourke's production set in the 1980s, we decided to think of it as the summer dance anthem of the time. We used it in its full 1980s-style recorded version for the ending of the play when the couples reconciled, but in the scene in which it originally appears (and where it is sung by the character Balthazar) we treated it in a much softer way more akin to a ballad. Here we stripped it down using only acoustic guitar and voice, which helped to keep the lyric clear. In the scene, Don Pedro actually calls for the song, so its function is diegetic. The instrumentation had to reflect this reality. From a story point of view, the song helps to paint Benedick's reluctance to the idea of romance alongside the feckless nature of all men. Technically, it is used to set up Benedick's hiding and detection, which will be exploited in the impending 'gulling' scene. Here is an example of how songs can have a dual function, thematic and narrative (illustrating the foibles of love) or technical and mechanical (allowing Don Pedro and co the set-up for their plan of mischief against Benedick). One imagines any technical aspects would also be useful here due to the practicalities of the Elizabethan theatre, which had no curtain or shifting scenery.

Case Study: *Hay Fever* in the West End

Sometimes a playwright will suggest a type of song but not provide any lyrics or further guidelines. In Noël Coward's *Hay Fever* Judith Bliss '*plays and sings a little French song*'. That's it for the stage directions, but there are brief clues from the surrounding dialogue of the song's nature:

> JUDITH (*rising from the piano*). It's pretty, isn't it?
>
> RICHARD. Perfectly enchanting.

It seems surprising to me that Noël Coward, being the expert songwriter that he was, didn't pen this 'little French song' or, if he did, didn't publish it in the playtext. Perhaps he merely chose to leave it up to each individual production to approach it in an appropriate way for their leading actress, or maybe he did write it and it got lost somewhere along the way.

In any case, when a song like this needs to be included, you have several things to consider from a practical point of view. Are you going to write something new or find an existing song that will be appropriate? Is your leading actress a capable singer? Do you have a real piano on stage? Can your actress play the piano? If not, how are you going to effectively fake it? If you're going to write a new song, are you going to write new lyrics or find a French lyric or a piece of poetry to set?

When I wrote the music for Lindsay Posner's 2015 West End production of this play, our leading actress Felicity Kendal didn't play the piano, but could sing and became wonderful at miming the piano part. Our associate director helped me to find an appropriate piece of French poetry which I cut down to a useful length and set to music in a way that wasn't too vocally challenging but was still interesting enough to warrant the line: 'Perfectly enchanting.' (Although, to be fair, that praise should be ascribed to the performance of the actress in question and not necessarily the song itself.) We positioned the piano upstage, but facing downstage so the piano keys were mostly obscured from the audience's view. The keys were dampened so they were still playable but silent, and our sound designer positioned a speaker so the piano sounds were coming from the right spot acoustically. Setting lyrics in languages that you don't speak can be a little tricky, so I always try to get a fluent or native speaker to record the words slowly for me to pick up the correct speech inflections and accent. I don't ever find it quite as satisfactory as writing in English as I'm still unaware of exactly how the musical setting sounds to the native speaker's ear.

Case Study: *Trelawny of the Wells* at the Donmar Warehouse

Sometimes a director will ask for a new song that doesn't appear in the original script. This can be for a number of reasons, but quite often it's a useful cover for a scene change. In the Donmar's production of Pinero's *Trelawny of the Wells*, the director Joe Wright asked me to find a historically appropriate song that an actress could sing accompanied by a barrel organ. Set around the theatres of 1860s London, it is a play about the birth of a more 'realist' style of drama (the drawing-room comedy) out of the melodramatic-theatre style that was popular at the time. This song was positioned to cover a large scene change from a theatrical boarding house to a conservative upper-class townhouse. Because the Donmar has a thrust stage, much of this scene change had to happen in full view of the audience. The song was staged with the performer being aware of and able to interact with what was going on around her, scene-change-wise. She had the tricky task of trying to hold the audience's attention and entertain them while lots of action happened all around her. To help with this I tried to find a song with a story the audience could follow and with enough events (stops, changes of feel and tempo) to keep it interesting. After a bit of research I found a suitable song from the period that I adjusted slightly and rearranged to be played on a barrel organ that could fit within our world. Traditionally, barrel organs are 'played' by a person turning a crank or by clockwork driven by weights or springs.[41] Music is encoded onto wooden barrels, cylinders or paper reels. These days you can get MIDI-controlled barrel organs, but due to the changeable nature and limited time constraints of a technical rehearsal, I decided the safest option would be to build a fake barrel-organ case and put a speaker inside it. This meant that I could record the organ music using a software sampler and change and edit it to my heart's content (as opposed to being stuck with whichever version of the song we managed to get engraved or punched onto the barrel or reel). It also allowed me to change the quality and level of the sound. It's always best to keep control over as many elements as you can, and there was no way to know how loud a real barrel organ would sound in a fully populated theatre without trying it out. Our method meant that we could balance the level of the singer (who was discreetly mic'd for this moment only) with the barrel organ and the acoustics of the space, and keep the whole process fluid over the period of the run with the addition of a sound engineer to mix it live.

This is an example of a song which provided a tonal shift for a play, but didn't progress plot or have any narrative or dramatic function (apart from a shift in location).

Case Study: *The Recruiting Officer* at the Donmar Warehouse

In *The Recruiting Officer*, a song we added, based on a seventeenth-century poem by Anne Finch, helped to contextualise a scene and set up a contrast for the next. At this point in the play a simple countryman is duped into joining the army. His best friend, knowing this, and in an act of incredible beneficence, decides to sign up alongside him, knowing they will both probably die in action. I found it an extraordinarily moving scene, illustrating the power of friendship. In contrast, the following scene is between two friendly noblemen sharing their grievances about their haphazard love lives.

The dynamic contrast between the scenes is very clear but, after such an emotional section, it felt like there needed to be a moment for an audience to absorb what (from a thematic perspective) was an important scene in the play. Also, from a practical point of view it was useful to have some music to cover the various actors' entrances and exits. This song provided a useful bridge between the extremes of circumstance, providing subtext to the first and juxtaposition to the second.

The poetry itself, though appropriate in its date and subject matter, needed to be edited a bit to suit our purposes (we replaced 'Ardelia' with 'dear friend'). Having said that, we couldn't have found a more fitting lyric. I can only hope that the airing of this verse in whatever context would be pleasing to the author almost three hundred years after its publication.

Here is the original version of the poem:

Friendship Between Ephelia and Ardelia
by Anne Finch, Countess of Winchilsea

Eph. What Friendship is, Ardelia show.
Ard. 'Tis to love, as I love you.
Eph. This account, so short (tho' kind)
Suits not my inquiring mind.
Therefore farther now repeat:
What is Friendship when complete?
Ard. 'Tis to share all joy and grief;
'Tis to lend all due relief
From the tongue, the heart, the hand;
'Tis to mortgage house and land;
For a friend be sold a slave;
'Tis to die upon a grave,
If a friend therein do lie.
Eph. This indeed, tho' carried high,
This, tho' more than e'er was done
Underneath the rolling sun,
This has all been said before.
Can Ardelia say no more?
Ard. Words indeed no more can show:
But 'tis to love, as I love you.

Inevitably, the song was further cut in rehearsals and previews (which happens a lot), meaning it was even shorter for the run of the play, but the essence of it was still there:

What friendship is, dear friend, do show.
'Tis to love, as I love you.
'Tis to share all joy and grief;
'Tis to lend all due relief
From the tongue, the heart, the hand;
'Tis to mortgage house and land;
Words indeed no more can show:
But 'tis to love, as I love you.

Occasionally a director may ask you to set some verse or even prose to music to create a sung moment where there never was one. Sometimes it won't progress the plot but merely frame a moment or a feeling. Melody can be 'the index and the natural result of definite emotional conditions with vague results in the world of action. It looks to no consequences, it is complete in its own paradise. A song sung naturally gives us a picture, not an incident.' So said our wise friend H.B. Lathrop.[42]

Case Study: *Coriolanus* at the Donmar Warehouse

In Josie Rourke's production of *Coriolanus*, the last two scenes were performed out of order so that the scene describing the family's return to Rome (normally Act Five, Scene Five) was performed as an epilogue after Coriolanus' death. This short scene (only seven lines long) is normally spoken by an unnamed senator. We decided to musicalise it and have it recorded by a young chorister (echoing the voice of Coriolanus' young son). This was the underscore for the final tableau: Coriolanus' dead and bloodied body hanging centre stage, celebratory petals falling from the sky and the solemn appearance of his mother upstage. A common criticism of the play is that you cannot empathise with the lead character, but in this moment we were able to help the audience empathise with both the reluctant anti-hero and his family.

The melody was written to be sparse and haunting, but I believe that it was the purity of a child's singing voice after so much turmoil, bloodied action and anguish (and indeed electronica music) that released the tension of the evening and allowed it to dissipate in an extraordinary way.

Suffice to say, it can be harder to set prose that has not been intended to be sung – lines are of varying lengths and there are no rhyme schemes to speak of. Nevertheless, musicalising text like this (although uncommon) can be highly effective if for a good reason.

 **CORIOLANUS c**

More on Foreign-language Lyrics

Sometimes if you do decide to find a lyric rather than write one you may have to do a good deal of editing to fit it to your purpose. You may even have to translate it to another language.

Case Study: *The Two Gentlemen of Verona* for the Royal Shakespeare Company

In Simon Godwin's production of *The Two Gentlemen of Verona* I was asked to add in a whole new song and dance sequence at the top of Act Two, Scene Four. This was a contemporary-styled production set in modern-day Italy. At this moment we needed to create as big a contrast as possible between the previous scenes in a sleepy rural Verona and the big city lights and spectacle of Milan. As the text in the show was (obviously) Shakespearean English, it made sense that I should find a lyric of a similar era to set for the party music. Because we wanted to increase the feeling of alienation in Milan, using actual Italian (for an English audience) felt like an interesting ruse. As this was a set piece within the world of the play but outside the original text I decided to find a translation of a Shakespearean sonnet in seventeeth-century Italian. Using Italian lyrics really helped to give the music a particularly European flavour and alongside an energised Eurobeat musical influence provided this section of the play a fresh vigour that felt suitably modern.

 **THE TWO GENTLEMEN OF VERONA**

As previously mentioned, it's always best to get a native speaker to check over anything you do in a foreign language. It can be particularly tricky if the text is in an ancient dialect. Pay particular attention to where stresses fall and which syllables are accented. This will help you to work out the shape of the melody from the words rather than trying to make a lyric fit a melody (particularly one in a foreign language). You may of course ask, why bother? Why go to all the effort when it's likely no one will understand what the singer is singing anyway? But I think it's good to feel passionate about the small details, even if nobody else notices.

Direction from Authors

Sometimes a playwright will quite clearly pass the buck. Here is one of my all-time favourite stage directions, from George Farquhar's *The Recruiting Officer*. In the middle of Act Three, Scene One:

> *Enter* ROSE *singing what she pleases.*

Fair enough.

Writing Your Own Lyrics

When approaching writing lyrics for songs in plays, it can be useful to consider this: the *craft* surrounding the writing of the lyric needs to belong to the world of the genre it references or the character singing it. Different genres of music (and in some respect different writers) obey their own rules of lyric writing and have varying levels of discipline about what is acceptable as a rhyme. You can examine rhyme schemes in the same way you can break down melodic phrasing, by assigning each different end-rhyme a letter, but obviously, as with music, there are complex patterns, rhyme schemes and syntax uses to consider.

In his book *Finishing the Hat*, Stephen Sondheim is helpfully clear on the differences between writing poetry and lyrics:

> Poetry is an art of concision, lyrics of expansion. Poems depend on packed images, on resonance and juxtaposition, on density. Every reader absorbs a poem at his own pace, inflecting it with his own rhythms, stresses and tone. The tempo is dictated less by what the poet intends than by the reader's comprehension... The poet may guide us with punctuation and layout and seduce us with the subtle abutment of words and sounds, but it is we who supply the musical treatment... Poetry can be set to music gracefully... but the music benefits more from the poem which gives it structure than the poem does from the music, which often distorts not only the poet's phrasing but also the language itself, clipping syllables short or extending them into near-unintelligibility. Music straitjackets a poem and prevents it from breathing on its own, whereas it liberates a lyric. Poetry doesn't need music; lyrics do.[43]

Lyrics only truly make sense when they are set to music. They are written to be, and only complete when they are, sung. Because of this, lyrics on the page tend to look quite stale and pedestrian. As Sondheim says, 'In theatrical fact, it is usually the plainer and flatter lyric that soars poetically when infused with music.'[44] Therefore don't examine your lyrics without considering how they work in tandem with the music.

I have heard second hand that the lyricist Tim Rice sets his lyrics to tunes of his own, just to hear 'if they sing' – before wryly noting a few seconds of disappointment when he hears them set by the proper composer (i.e. Elton John).

Lyrical Terms

There are a variety of techniques, structures and terminologies used when examining lyrics. Here is a list of useful terms or phrases to look out for:

- **Metre**: The rhythmic pattern of stressed and unstressed syllables.
- **Foot**: The smallest unit of metre made up of stressed or unstressed syllables. The arrangement and repetition of feet make up a line in poetry.
- **Stress**: Where the syllabic accent falls in a word.
- **Stanza**: A group of lines in poetry constituting a verse. Or in song form a verse, bridge or chorus.
- **True or Perfect Rhymes**: Phrases whose accented syllables sound alike except for the consonant sounds that precede them. Can be masculine or feminine rhymes, such as *spoke/broke* or *legion/region.*
- **Masculine Rhyme**: The rhyme that occurs in a final stressed syllable, as in *pair/ chair* or *address/confess*.
- **Feminine Rhyme**: The rhyme that occurs between stressed syllables that are followed by unstressed syllables, as in *fainted/sainted* or *measure/treasure*.
- **Near or False Rhymes**: These come in two brands – assonance and consonance.
- **Assonance**: Vowel sounds are alike but with different consonants, as in *dome/drone*.
- **Consonance or Slant Rhyme**: Consonants are alike but with different vowels, as in *blank/think*.
- **Identities**: Words that match both the final syllables and the consonants that introduce them, as in *vision/division*.

- **Internal Rhyme**: Rhymes that occur inside a line of verse, as in:

  When I see a fountain flow from a mountain
  Or see April showers bring flowers to May
  (*Dolly Parton/Willie Nelson*)

  Rhymes that appear in the middle of two different lines of verse, as in:

  I dim the lights and think about you
  Spend sleepless nights to think about you
  (*Stephen Sondheim*)

  Or when a word at the end of a line rhymes with one in the middle of the following line, as in:

  Moon River, wider than a mile
  I'm crossing you in style some day
  (*Johnny Mercer*)

- **Alliteration**: Repetition of similar or identical sounds at the beginnings of words, as in *Whisper words of wisdom* (*Lennon/McCartney*).
- **Metonymy**: Substituting the name of something for an attribute or idea commonly associated with that thing, as in *the big smoke* instead of *London*.
- **Metaphor**: The application of a word or a phrase to something to which it is not literally applicable, making an implicit comparison, as in *her glassy eyes* or *sea of troubles*.
- **Simile**: Two unlike things compared by a figurative example, as in *her eyes were like glass* or *fast as a cheetah*.
- **Personification**: Attributing human characteristics to anything other than a human being, as in *the wind blew angrily*.
- **Prosody**: The way the syllables of a piece of text are set to the melody, rhythm or phrasing of a piece of music. When done well ensures the correct accents of text and music correlate.

- **Melisma**: The singing of several notes on the same syllable, e.g. the word *shame* in 'I Dreamed a Dream' from *Les Misérables*.

As you absorb the music and lyrical content of a particular genre or artist, look out for their usage of the above techniques. You may begin to see patterns in their writing that will help you to create some parameters for yourself when you begin to write in that style.

Modes

In his 2001 article 'Understanding and Writing Lyrics', Sam Inglis delves into the concept of 'modes' in lyric writing. The mode of a poem or lyric implies certain things about the narrator; to whom they are speaking and what effect their words are to have on the listener.[45] It may be useful to have a look at the three main modes we come across in song writing: the Lyric Mode, the Dramatic Mode and the Narrative Mode.

Inglis describes a lyric being in the Lyric Mode if 'its primary purpose is to express the emotions of the narrator, and to bring about a particular emotional response from the listener'.[46] Often (but not exclusively) used in the present tense, the Lyric Mode always uses a first-person narrator. Although commonly used to describe the emotions of the narrator, it can be used to describe their circumstance or other non-emotional details about them. Common examples of this include 'Homeward Bound' by Simon and Garfunkel, 'New York State of Mind' by Billy Joel, and 'I Think It's Going to Rain Today' by Randy Newman.

The Dramatic Mode is described as consisting of 'a speech or address made to someone or something... [it] takes the form of a message being delivered to a specific thing, person or group of people – it is a verse intended to tell someone something'.[47] Examples of songs written in this mode include 'That Don't Impress Me Much' sung by Shania Twain, 'We Will Rock You' by Queen, and 'Cry Me a River' sung by Julie London.

Inglis elaborates:

> The message of the song can be directed not at any one person, but at a group of people, or even at everyone... it can be directed at an animal, or at a place, or at an inanimate object, as in songs like The Kinks' 'Lazy Old Sun' (from *Something Else*). Elton John's 'Candle in the Wind', in both its versions, is a special kind of dramatic verse called an 'apostrophe', in which the speech is directed at someone or something known to be either abstract, non-existent or dead. While songs in the dramatic mode can employ descriptions of events that happened in the past, or will happen in the future, they are written as if addressing the subject now.[48]

Songs in the Narrative Mode 'just tell a story, rather than using stories to explain the narrator's feelings or to convey a message... you have a choice between using a first-person narrator, describing events as though happening to him or her, and a third-person or "omniscient" narrator.'[49] Songs in this mode include 'Don't Stand So Close to Me' by The Police, 'Livin' on a Prayer' by Bon Jovi, and 'Circle of Life' by Tim Rice and Elton John.

Rhyme

There is one particular genre of music that requires a particular amount of detail be paid to lyrical craft, and that is musical theatre. As the leading contemporary lyricist and composer in that field, Stephen Sondheim has become notorious for his rigorous discipline for perfect rhyme. In *Finishing the Hat*, Sondheim quotes the composer-lyricist Craig Carnelia:

> True rhyming is a necessity in the theater, as a guide for the ear to know what it has just heard. Our language is so complex and difficult, and there are so many similar words and sounds that mean different things, that it's confusing enough without using near rhymes that only acquaint the ear with a vowel... [A near rhyme is] not useful to the primary purpose of a lyric, which is to be heard, and it teaches the ear not to trust or disregard a lyric, to not listen, to simply let the music wash over you.[50]

If you are writing a song that falls into the camp of contemporary musical theatre, it is wise to observe the guidelines of the genre as best as you can. With theatre in general, if you want an audience to hear and understand a lyric it needs to be as clear as possible. Audiences only get one shot at hearing a lyric (unlike in a pop record when they can listen to it over and over again to absorb meaning), but they also get the added help of having an actor delivering the lines with intention. Hopefully an actor will help with clarity, but perfect rhyming is a much better way to ensure your lyric is heard and understood. That's not to say that there are not songs in musicals that use false rhymes, but they tend to be much better suited to the world of pop, rap, R&B and rock music. As long as you know what the common traits (I won't say rules) are of the genre you're writing in, then you should be able to tackle any challenge that comes your way.

Act Three:

Process

*'The old idea of a composer suddenly having
a terrific idea and sitting up all night
to write it is nonsense. Night-time is for sleeping.'*

Benjamin Britten

Rehearsing

The Meet-and-Greet

The morning of day one of rehearsals can be an exciting and sometimes slightly awkward time. Usually for the first half-hour on the first morning, the rehearsal room is full of people who are either directly working on the production (creatives, actors and production staff) or are attached to the building (if you're working in a producing theatre) or the production company (if you're working for a commercial producer). Sometimes you'll even see the financial backers for the production at this meeting. This session is an opportunity to meet the people you'll be working with, but there are sometimes so many it can be a little bewildering. Everyone is a bit nervous for the first day of rehearsals. The more experienced you get at these meetings, the less awkward they become, and pretty soon you'll come across familiar faces from previous projects. The entertainment industry is relatively small, all things considered. Carrying casual conversation and introducing yourself to new people are useful skills to learn for any career, but will be called upon regularly if you wish to sustain a career as a composer in the theatre. Meet-and-greets, press-night parties, production meetings, recording sessions, rehearsal rooms, and theatres in general will always bring you into contact with lots of new people and you must learn how to interact and hold your own in any situation.

Later in this book we will address how to get jobs and sustain work, but (surprise surprise), more than any other industry, showbusiness is about people. People will give you jobs, people will work with you, people will pay to see your work, people will support your artistic endeavours. Make sure you look people in the eye and be genuine. Everything else is up to you.

After the initial milling around and sometimes (if you're lucky) tea, coffee and pastries, the next step is typically to encourage the group to form a circle and have people introduce themselves one by one. Nobody ever expects you to remember anyone's name or job title, but it's an effective ice-breaker and gives you a general idea of what everyone is there for and how many people it takes to make a production happen.

The Model Presentation

Sometimes, and this depends very much on the director (and possibly the designer's schedule), a model-box showing will follow the meet-and-greet. Occasionally this is open for everyone and sometimes only the cast, stage management and creative team. Depending on how much pre-rehearsal preparation you have been required to do, this may very well be your first chance to see the model box of the set in full. The director and designer will normally talk everyone through the design choices and answer the company's questions. These sessions tend to be a little more concentrated on the acting company, and you will normally get plenty of opportunities to see the model box privately later. Don't be afraid to get involved if you want, but also bear in mind that questions you may have will not necessarily concern others at this meeting. It's better to reserve particulars for later when you can talk to the director or designer alone.

As well as the model-box presentation, designers sometimes have costume sketches to show as well. Take all this information in and absorb as much design influence as you can.

The First Readthrough

After another quick coffee, the company will usually sit down around a large table in the rehearsal room and read the play. Sometimes the model-box presentation will be skipped and this readthrough will happen directly after the meet-and-greet. (Very occasionally, the meet-and-greet is postponed and only the core acting company, stage management and creative team will be there on day one.) This first read-through is a very important part of your process as a composer. This is the first opportunity you have to hear the play spoken by the actors who will be on stage every night, and although it should not be considered a performance it will give you a good indication of how it might sound.

Sometimes directors may take a different approach. I've seen directors ask for a circle of music stands to be placed in the middle of the room, with the actors sat in a circle around them. When an actor enters a scene they stand up by the music stand (using it to support their script) and play the scene across the space to each other. This gives a certain level of energy to the reading and also makes it clear who is actually in the scene. Sometimes, if the language is difficult, it helps to get the essence of the action of the scene if the actors read standing up. This is very useful for you as a composer as it allows you to gain a sense of how a scene might feel when mobilised and energised, which will impact the tone of the scene and therefore the music.

Each director tends to have his or her own way of tackling the first readthrough, and it can vary from play to play. Some directors don't ask actors to read their own parts on the first reading. Instead what they do is go round the table getting each person to read the next speech, stage direction or chunk of lines (if it's a particularly long speech). This negates any pressure to give a performance and enables everyone to absorb the text at face value. Bear in mind that if you are sat at the table for the readthrough, you may be asked to join in with this process. If you've decided to stick around for rehearsals, I would suggest that you join in where appropriate. If you can get a thorough understanding of the play (which is what a lot of this part of the process is about) then the music you write will be much better informed and integrated into the final production.

I once worked on a Shakespeare play where the director asked whoever was reading around the table to paraphrase what they had just read and give a modern English version of it. There was no pressure to get anything correct necessarily (the whole company supported each other through tricky bits), but it was a great way to begin to comprehend what was actually being said and a good incentive not to switch your brain off.

The Music Plot

If you haven't already marked in where you think music might fit in the play, the first reading is a good time to do this. I normally make notes in the margins and highlight sections that either talk directly about music or infer that there might be some required. I'll underline moments that might warrant the support of underscore, and mark pages where these notes are. Even just folding down the corners of relevant pages at this point is useful. After you've made these marks (and I normally do this before the first reading) you can create a document that labels all the music cues you think you're likely to need and reference them by scene or page number. I call this a 'music plot'. You can also make up names for scenes that might help you to remember their content at a quick glance and share them with your fellow creatives. Some directors go one step further and officially name the scenes for everyone in the rehearsal process. This means that instead of talking about 'Act Two, Scene One', for instance, you can talk about 'Awaiting Coriolanus'.

Case Study: *Coriolanus* at the Donmar Warehouse

1.1 Opening
Boy singing leads into Romans talking in Latin/graffiti.
Pg 2. Opening music segue into **Belly Speech**
Pg 5. Enter Martius

(1.1b)
Pg 7. Enter Cominius, Titus Lartius and other Senators, Brutus and Sicinia.

1.2
Music and whispered Volsce Latin voices.
Pg 10. **Volscian Senate**. Enter Aufidius, Lieutenant and a Senator.

1.3
Pg 12. **Women At Home**

1.4
Pg 16. **Corioles.** Enter with a drum and colours.
Pg 17. Drums from far off. Swords clash. Battle for Corioles. Alarum. The Romans are beat back to their trenches. Another alarum. The Volsces fly and Martius follows them to their gates.
Pg 18. Alarum continues. Re-enter Titus Lartius.
Re-enter Martius bleeding.
They fight and all enter the city.

1.5
Pg 19. **Corioles.** Enter Romans with spoils.
Alarum continues still far off.
Enter Martius and Titus Lartius with a trumpet.
Big noise from far off.

1.6
Pg 21. **Battle Field.** Enter Cominius with soldiers.
Pg 23. They all shout and wave their swords.

1.7

Pg 24. **The Fight.** Alarum as in battle.
Enter Martius and Aufidius.
They fight.

1.8

Pg 25. **Coriolanus.** Flourish. Alarum. A retreat is sounded. Enter Cominius with the Romans, Martius with his arm in a scarf.
Pg 26. A long flourish. They all cry 'Martius! Martius!' cast up their caps and lances.
Flourish. Trumpets sound and drums.

1.9

Pg 28. **Curses.** Defeated Volscians. Enter Aufidius, bloody with two soldiers.

2.1

Pg 30. **Awaiting Coriolanus.** Enter Menenius with Sicinia and Brutus.
Pg 34. A shout and flourish. Build under Volumnia: 'These are the ushers of Martius… ' Big stage-wipe of cast. A sennet. Trumpets sound. Enter Cominius, Titus Lartius and Coriolanus.
Flourish.
Pg 36. Flourish. Cornets. Brutus and Sicinia come forward.

2.1a

Pg 39. **Triumph.**

2.2

Pg 39. **A Senate.**
Pg 42. Flourish of cornets. Exeunt all but Sicinia and Brutus.

2.3a

Pg 43. **Market Place.** Enter citizens, Brutus and Sicinia.
Enter Coriolanus in the gown of humility with Menenius.

2.3b

Pg 47. **Tribunes Plot.** Re-enter citizens with Sicinia and Brutus.

3.1
Pg 50. **It Kicks Off.** Cornets. Enter Coriolanus, Menenius and others.
Pg 56. Enter a rabble of Citizens.

3.2
Pg 60. **At Home.** Enter Coriolanus and Patricians.

3.3
Pg 65. **Banish.** Enter Sicinia and Brutus.
Pg 66. Enter Coriolanus, Menenius and Cominius with Senators and Patricians.

4.1
Pg 71. **Farewell.** Enter Coriolanus, Volumnia, Virgilia, Menenius, Cominius, with the young nobility of Rome.

4.2
Pg 73. **Volumnia vs Tribunes.** Enter Sicinia and Brutus. Enter Volumnia, Virgilia and Menenius.

4.3
Pg 76. **Antium.** Enter Coriolanus in mean apparel, disguised and muffled.

4.4
Pg 78. **Aufidius' House.** Music within. Enter a Servingman.

4.5
Pg 84. **Bad News for Rome.** Enter Sicinia and Brutus.
Pg 89. Enter a troop of Citizens.

4.6
Pg 91. **Aufidius' Beef.** Enter Aufidius and his Lieutenant.

5.1
Pg 93. **Cominius Spurned.** Enter Menenius, Sicinia, Brutus and others.

5.2
Pg 96. **Menenius Spurned.** Two sentinels on guard. Enter Menenius.

5.3a
Pg 100. **'O Mother Mother'.** Enter Coriolanus, Aufidius and others.
Enter in mourning habits, Virgilia, Volumnia, Young Martius, Valeria and attendants.
Pg 105. Holds her by the hand, silent.

5.3b
Pg 107. **Sacrifice.** Coriolanus is slain.
A dead march sounded.

5.4
Pg 108. **Rome's Saviour.** Enter two senators with Volumnia, Virgilia, Valeria, etc., followed by Patricians and others.
A flourish with drums and trumpets.

As you can see, this is an early document in the working process that mostly just marks the set-up for each scene, character entrances, and where music could potentially go. Sometimes I have marked a note for myself about what it says about music in the script. This document is rough and tends to be for your eyes only, although it is often useful to share it with the sound designer. This is only the beginning of your process and as such, no potential ideas should be completely filtered out. Looking back at this document it is apparent that at this stage the idea for the ending (where we heard a young boy sing instead of the 'flourish with drums and trumpets') hadn't happened yet. Much of the music that ended up in the show will not have been considered when this document was drawn up, but a lot of the preliminary geography is there to see.

After the readthrough, depending on the director and the play itself, you'll either leave and let the actors settle in with the director together or, as I like to do quite often, stick around and watch the process develop.

If there is not much in the way of music, or it doesn't provide much of a narrative function in the play, you may be able to head off after the readthrough and look after your other projects. For the sake of this book, I'll describe the process mostly from the perspective of those jobs where I've stuck around for the first week or so of rehearsals and examined the play alongside the company. Some directors do not like people outside of the cast watching their rehearsal process, which is fair enough. Make sure you know that it's okay for you to be there. A lot of directors love the extra input you can bring to the process.

Table Work

Depending on the play and the director's process, they may wish to dive straight in, get the actors on their feet right away and start staging the first scene (or any scene for that matter). Normally, though, there is anything between an afternoon to a week's worth of table work that has to happen first. This is an opportunity to explore the plot, background and social context of the play, share the collective knowledge of the group and discuss in depth the issues it raises. Sometimes you may even get to meet a historian or scholar who specialises in the issues or historical context of the play. This is very useful for a composer and a part I particularly enjoy. Not only do you begin to formulate ideas about tone, transitions and potential musical style, you can start more fully to comprehend the piece you're working on and the period in which it's set. Sometimes you won't be thinking directly about what function the music will have as you go through this process. It's enough just to absorb everything that is going on around you, learn about the play, but also get to know the actors who will be performing it. This is a good way to ensure that when you do eventually write the music, it will fit with these particular actors in this specific production.

Sometimes, if music plays a large part in your production, the director may ask you to talk in a little more detail about the style you are planning to write. He may even ask you to give an informal presentation about the history of the music and its context with regards to the play. This doesn't happen often, but several times I have given such mini-presentations and found it a really good exercise that forces me to do comprehensive research and think a great deal about why I'm planning to make the music choices I am. Also, it can be good to get those ideas (and they are only ideas at this point) out into the open at an early stage: just airing them in the private surroundings of the rehearsal room will tell you a lot about whether you're on the right path, and you should never underestimate the input of the acting company. Of course, the choices you make will be decided in collaboration with the director, but often actors will share something that they've picked up from a source you would never normally have uncovered. After years of going through the process of rehearsing shows, actors bring an incredibly wide-ranging volume of knowledge to the table read. Absorb as much of this as you can.

The main point of this exercise is to share with the company the history and style of the type of music you plan to use in the show. If there is a large amount of music to be integrated into the play, it's a good way to ensure that everyone understands where it is coming from. In the past, amongst others, I have given a potted history of eighteenth-century French opera and twentieth-century Irish folk music – and in both cases the exercise of sharing it with the group led to useful and unexpected discoveries.

Blocking

However long the table work lasts, the next stage is likely to be the start of the process of 'blocking' or staging the play. This is the part that is normally the least useful for you to observe, so it's likely you won't need to attend these sessions. It's always useful to keep in close contact with the rehearsal room, especially if there is some music that needs integrating early on, but ordinarily this is the point where you should start seriously thinking about stepping away from the rehearsal room and getting ready to compose.

Time Management

Rehearsal processes vary in length from a couple of weeks to a couple of months (or sometimes more) and it will be up to you to structure your schedule outside the rehearsal room so that you can write and deliver the music at the appropriate times. At the very least, you will be in weekly contact with the rehearsal room via the production meeting (which we will cover shortly) but, depending on the director and the piece, you may be in and out frequently to observe rehearsals or try out music cues.

In the later stages of the rehearsal period it is quite common for the creative team to be invited to watch rehearsals. You should make the most of it. You can request to sit in earlier than this, but bear in mind that some actors don't like the added pressure of extra people in the room while they're still in the infant stages of their process. It is part of a director's job to protect their actors from any undue distraction or stress, so it's best to take their lead on this. Also bear in mind that because directors tend to be very busy, the best way to keep in touch with everything happening in the rehearsal room is through the stage-management team.

Stage Management

The stage-management team are the unsung heroes of the theatrical world. At the National Theatre's fiftieth-anniversary gala performance there was an apposite and poignant moment at the curtain call when the entire stage management and backstage crew joined the actors on stage. Normally stage management do not get a bow, they do not get applause or huge salaries, but they are on the front line of everything that goes on in both the rehearsal room and the theatre. Members of stage management can be your best allies during the whole process of putting a show on stage. Often they share jobs, or two or more jobs are amalgamated into one, but the following is a brief lowdown of the main players in the stage-management team:

Company Manager/Company Stage Manager (CSM): This is the person who is in charge of the performing and creative company on a daily basis. They usually set up an office next door to the rehearsal room and deal with the day-to-day running of the rehearsal room, health and safety, scheduling, admin and company well-being, as well as liaising with production and creative teams and sending out rehearsal calls every night for the next day. They are in charge of running a technical rehearsal and making sure the show runs smoothly for the duration of its performance schedule.

Deputy Stage Manager (DSM): This is the person who works closely with the director in the rehearsal room, recording blocking, prompting actors (being 'on the book'), and generating rehearsal notes to pass to different departments. During the performance they are in charge of calling all cues (lights, sound, music, video, flies, automation, actors to stage for their next scene). This is known as 'calling the show'. They will create a 'prompt copy' of the script for the show which details the cue points for all technical aspects, should they be unable to be at a particular performance.

Assistant Stage Manager (ASM): The ASM works in conjunction with the other members of stage management, commonly sourcing and maintaining props for rehearsals and performances, setting the stage before the performance and assisting during scene changes or transitions. They are often found in the rehearsal room or stage manager's office helping to keep all aspects of either rehearsal or performance running smoothly. On larger-scale shows you may also find Technical ASMs, ASM Book Cover or Wardrobe ASMs, who all have slightly more specific responsibilities during the running of a show.

Production Manager: The production manager deals with all of the creative members of the team, running production meetings, handling individual budgets, costing all production elements and managing the overall budget. (As a composer, however, you will usually deal with either the producer or the general manager regarding your music budget.) The production manager works with the designer and scenery builders to ensure the set is completed on schedule and to the correct specifications, and will be in charge of its maintenance in the theatre until press night, after which it is handed over to the theatre staff. They are also in charge of the technical rehearsal and preview schedule, ensuring all departments have the time and resources they need to complete their work. They will run 'technical notes' after the performance during previews, where the director, creative and technical departments can give and receive notes based on that particular performance.

In the Rehearsal Room

Sometimes directors will ask you to write music for rehearsal-room purposes that will not end up in the show. I was once asked by a director to write a musical response to each scene in a play, just for rehearsal purposes. These small piano pieces were never intended for the final production, and weren't even in the style of the eventual score, but were merely designed to encourage the mutual understanding of tone and mood in each scene and hopefully to provide an 'opening-up' point for discussion, as a way of approaching the play from a different angle. I spent no more than a few hours writing this music and then played it to the company in an informal setting, but it was a useful exercise in forcing an interaction with, and interpretation of, the drama from my own perspective. These piano scores were added to the company research that was posted on the walls of the rehearsal room for inspiration and reference for the duration of the rehearsal process.

Writing in the Room

Occasionally I have written a score in the rehearsal room. This is slightly unorthodox as normally I need to take some time away and work quietly on my own, but when we staged *Coriolanus* at the Donmar the volume of music and the manner in which it was devised alongside the choreography meant there simply wasn't time to go home and think about it. I often worked in a separate room with the choreographer and some of the cast, workshopping ideas for how transitions or battle sequences could be achieved on the relatively small stage of the Donmar. As the score was mainly electronica, I was able to produce basic templates for moments (even just in tempo and structure) on a laptop quite quickly, and use these as placeholders in the rehearsal room. Any spare time was used to expand these templates and create a score proper out of them. This was a pretty daring way to work, but was the only option I could see being at all productive. Had I spent time crafting templates for the choreographer away from the rehearsal room, I would have been unable to keep up with the constantly shifting ideas that were being developed to tackle the tricky stagecraft.

You have to be thick-skinned to write music in the theatre as elements get changed and cut constantly. The process for *Coriolanus* was even more exposing as I was frequently composing 'on the fly'. Being a part of the rehearsal room early in the rehearsal period helped me to be at ease with the acting company, and they likewise with me. When you're working in a supportive environment like that, you can produce work that is very much 'in progress' and not feel overly anxious about being judged. Everyone in the room is working towards a mutual goal – to make the show the best it can be. It is in no one's interest to be hypercritical or unsupportive. Of course, sometimes you create more work for yourself by being very much a part of the messiness of a show's creation, but I personally think it's worth it for the end result. Being there at an idea's conception will render your score a much more integral part of the fabric of the piece than if you'd not become so involved and had written the whole score afterwards.

The Composer as Choir Master

Sometimes a play will require a piece of music to be played or a song to be sung by the entire acting company. This is a different scenario to working with actor-musicians who are accustomed to performing music. Some actors are very musical and some are not, but occasionally the production will call for everyone to perform together. Most commonly, this is a song. If a director is aware early in the process that they will require their cast to sing (sometimes it will only be an idea developed in the rehearsal room) they are likely to ask you to conduct a singing session with the company early on: probably in the first week. If you are involved in a large-scale production with lots of live music, there is a chance that you will be working with a musical director who will take the reins in moments like this, but it's most likely that you, as the 'music expert' in the room, will have to run this session. Some composers dislike this intensely, as they don't have a lot of experience directly working with actors, conducting singing calls or running a rehearsal room for a session. I was lucky to spend several of the early years of my career working as a musical director, so I'm accustomed to running singing warm-ups and teaching vocal harmonies. If it has been a while since I last ran a session, though, it can still be a slightly nerve-racking thing to sum up the energy for. Some actors can be very forthcoming with their refusal to participate in anything musical, so be aware who is comfortable and who is clearly not. Try not to push anyone into anything that has the potential to make him or her feel uncomfortable in front of the group (particularly in the early part of the process).

You will normally want to start your singing call with a vocal warm-up. This is not just a good way to warm the voice (and wake everyone up, if it's the start of the day), but also an opportunity for the cast to sing en masse with no pressure to be any good. No one should judge anyone's singing ability based on a vocal warm-up, it's the vocal equivalent of stretching. Warm-ups are good for breaking down inhibitions and letting the vocal energy expand and fill the space. Make sure you go into these sessions with a warm-up plan: a series of vocal exercises you know how to play on the piano in a variety of keys that are simple enough to teach as you go, but complex or stretching enough to make worthwhile over the course of a rehearsal period. If you do regular warm-ups, the company will get to know your exercises and hopefully their vocal skills will develop over time. As well as vocal conditioning, it's a good idea to share some fun tongue-twisters to get tongues moving and brains engaged, and to keep the warm-up light and energised. It is also worthwhile to introduce a few new exercises every now and then to prevent the warm-up from getting stale.

If your first vocal session is in the first week, it's unlikely that you will have written the music that is actually going to be in the show. Use these early sessions as a way to get to know the vocal timbres and capabilities of your cast. It is a good idea to bring a familiar song (that might be in the style of what you eventually plan to write) that you can teach to the group and use to try out various choral groupings or harmonies. Pick something simple but with the capacity to make more complex by harmonisation. I would suggest that you ask the members of the acting company if they are aware of their most comfortable vocal range. This doesn't mean they need to know anything specific, just if they think they are a high or a low singer. You have to assume that some of your company will not have done much in the way of choral singing so it's best to keep things very straightforward at this point. Group the company into the relevant harmony parts and teach them precisely but quickly. It is important in these introductory sessions that you maintain the energy in the room and keep everyone involved as much as possible. This session is not about getting a piece of music up to performance standard, it is about sussing out how confident and competent your singers are and what the vocal make-up of the group is. By the end of the session, try and get the whole company singing together (in harmony if possible) and run the song several times over. If you can make this a success, it will build the company's confidence in singing as a group. This will hold you in good stead for later on when you come to teach the actual music for the show.

Even after you have taught this music, you will have to maintain its quality over the course of rehearsals (including tech) and previews. Even once the production is up and running you may wish to watch it occasionally to keep an eye on things. Usually, however, there is at least one company member who is more experienced with music or singing who you can designate as 'vocal captain' to keep an ear on the group performance. This doesn't tend to be an official role, but quite often someone will volunteer for the job, and as long as you let the company as a whole know this person is going to act in this position, there shouldn't be any problems. Some acting companies have asked me to record a vocal warm-up so they can play it as part of their physical warm-up at every performance. If there is no musical director on the show every night, this is a good way for a company to keep their vocal performance in shape.

Production Meetings

These generally happen weekly during the rehearsal period, normally during a lunch hour. These meetings are for creative and technical staff only and are where the latest lowdown on each department's work is shared with the group. Production meetings are normally run by the production manager, who provides everyone with a proposed production schedule for technical rehearsals and previews. These meetings are great times to catch up with your sound designer if you haven't seen them in rehearsals and are a useful forum to share your technical music requirements with the group. If you are working with a live band then you will need to schedule band calls and specify technical needs for those. Obvious things like power sources, lamps and music stands are sometimes overlooked. Also, it may be that you need to discuss how a live band will appear on stage, where they are to be placed, how they are going to be mic'd, how they are going to travel from either a pit or a band platform to the stage, and other aspects of their involvement such as costume requirements or their rehearsal-period availability.

Be careful that you only share the necessary information in production meetings. All departments have a lot going on, so only contribute things that need to be heard by the group. Budget requirements and technical aspects for sound can normally be discussed privately with the general manager or production manager (both of whom control budgets) and the sound designer.

Typically the director will give a brief summation of how the week's rehearsals have been going and if they have any unfulfilled technical requirements for the rehearsal room. You may also be able to have a quick word with the director after this meeting about any music-related matters you have if you've not been actively in the rehearsal room. Be aware that if you have any more complex questions or matters to be discussed with the director, it's usually best to set up a separate meeting for this. Production meetings usually happen over a director's lunch hour and there are lots of people who will constantly want to ask them questions. Common sense, consideration and courtesy go a long way in maintaining good relationships with directors during the busy rehearsal period.

Runthroughs

Typically, towards the end of the final week of rehearsals, the company will run the play in the rehearsal room, sometimes referred to as a 'stagger-through'. Depending on your involvement, music may be very much a part of this run. Sometimes there will be more than one run of the play and you'll be invited to a specific runthrough. Usually there is an invited audience of necessary creative and technical staff who come to these runthroughs, and occasionally, if the play is ready and needs an audience reaction, the building staff will also be invited. These runthroughs happen without much technical support (as that is to come in the theatre). They are the amalgamation of all the rehearsal-room work of the preceding weeks, but are still far from the final product. They can give a good indication of work that still needs to be done and any issues that might arise once you're in the theatre. Normally after the final runthrough, the rehearsal room will be cleared and the entire company will transfer to the theatre to start tech week.

Even if you've been very involved with the rehearsal process, the music at this stage will still be some way off a final product. The more you've been around, the more likely you are to approach the tech week with confidence. Also, if you've become friendly with both the acting company and the technical team, the next part of the process will feel easier and much more pleasant. Things change so often during rehearsals, the temptation to procrastinate is huge, but try not to leave everything until the last minute. The rehearsal period may be over, but the real work is only just beginning.

Make sure you're as prepared as possible before you move into the theatre for the technical rehearsal.

Recording

As we've come to know, most scores for plays these days are pre-recorded. Let's examine the journey of the dots from the page through the recording and mixing process.

When to Record

We know that rehearsal periods vary greatly in length, but I find that if you wait until near the end of the rehearsal process, you're most likely to record music that is in tune with the production that has developed. Often you won't end up recording the score you thought you'd write on day one. Up until the final week it's quite normal for the score to remain rather fluid. I wouldn't suggest leaving the recording session to the very end of the last week, just in case something unexpected or disastrous occurs. I find it comforting to give myself a buffer of a few days just to be safe. Once you've committed to a recording date you can start to write the scores out in full.

Sometimes there are extra bits of recording that need to be accomplished that sit outside the realm of your score. The sound designer may need to record voice-overs or other sound effects, but this usually happens at a different time to the music session. We will cover running a recording session shortly, but you're normally very tight on time, so you don't want to allocate precious studio time to recording things not considered the 'score'. This may seem ungenerous, but it's realistic. Most sound designers and producers realise this and would never want to take time away from the recording of the music.

I have on occasion done completely separate recording sessions for elements of the score – some even that weren't strictly musical. The score for *Coriolanus* at the Donmar was mostly created electronically, but one of the features of the integration of the score and sound design was that we incorporated the spoken voices of the cast into the music. We had a recording session with selected members of the company (who were paid extra for this) in which we recorded lines from the play, Latin phrases and general crowd noise with different vocal qualities (shouting, chanting, whispering, etc.) and layered them up, using the human voice as an instrument built into the score. Using this as extra texture enabled us to give the sense of a much bigger crowd in the relatively small Donmar production and was an invaluable part of the final product. We also needed to record a solo chorister for the opening and closing moments, but knew we had too much to cover in the company vocal recording session so did this separately at a different time. It's important to be realistic about how much you can record in a single session, and when it comes to recording musicians the Musicians' Union have drawn up rules (which we will cover later).

Recording Studios

If you're recording in a professional studio, your recording dates will depend upon studio availability, so you will have to be able to work around this, and make sure you're prepared enough to be able to record earlier or later than you had hoped. It's normally best to pencil in the studio a couple of weeks in advance. Most recording studios have a 'pencilling' system that means a slot is reserved for you until you confirm. If someone else enquires about using the slot you have the right of first refusal. They are normally quite happy for you to change or cancel your booking if it has only been pencilled in. Depending on your relationship with the studio, and whether or not you've worked there before, they may require the producer to pay the entire fee upfront before the booking is confirmed. If you have a long-standing relationship with a studio, they often collect the fee after the session is completed, but sometimes a deposit will be due.

Recording studios are not cheap places to hire and, as we know, budgets for plays tend to be quite tight. You'll need to get a figure from your producer before you consider where you want (or are able) to record. Also, be realistic about the scope of your music. If you are only recording a couple of instruments you probably don't need a big fancy studio to do it in. Most studios bill by the hour with a minimum session length of three hours. There will also be a day rate for a period of twelve hours. Some also charge extra for 'ProTools hire', which goes towards the upkeep and upgrade of the ProTools Systems. In larger complexes with more than one studio, upgrades of the audio interfaces for each system are required, which can mean a number of interfaces in each studio, at a not inconsiderable cost. Every now and again the studio also needs to upgrade the computers themselves, so they keep the additional charge as a small offset towards the cost of running and maintaining the systems. All studios charge VAT on top of quoted prices so make sure you know exactly what the costs are upfront. (Producers should be able to reclaim the VAT.)

If you're considering using a studio that you haven't used before, and are unsure it will fulfil your size requirements, call up the studio manager who will be happy to advise you. In studio complexes that house more than one recording studio you may have several competing options.

One of the most crucial things to determine is the size and layout of the 'live room' in a recording studio. If you're only recording one instrument or singer, it won't really matter, but if you plan to record two or more instruments at the same time you need to make sure that a) they both fit and b) that their sound levels won't bleed uncontrollably into each other's mics. Some live rooms feature isolation booths (which are essentially different rooms) that mean you can record several instruments at the same time without sound spilling across channels. If there is only one live room and no extra isolation booths, acoustic screens can be placed between performers to allow better separation between them. These screens are made from sections of foam that slot together, or can be plywood screens filled with Rockwool or other absorption material covered with acoustic fabric.[51] They go some way towards isolating the microphones on different instruments, but ultimately it's likely you will get some sound spill across the channels on the recording. If you truly need isolated instruments you either have to record them separately or use an isolation booth.

Sound bleed, though annoying, tends not to be such a major problem with music for plays, as you'll inevitably want to use the full track with instruments playing together (if that's what you've written). A problem arises if you get to a later stage and want to use only one instrument line from a take. Unfortunately on a small budget that is a chance you'll have to take. If you want a natural-sounding performance with the instrumentalists in sync with each other it's best to get them to play together. If you are using a click track as a guide for the entirety of a cue then you can record instruments separately, but think carefully about this as it will vastly diminish your recording time. You're more likely to get better synchronisation between phrasing and breathing if instruments are recorded at the same time. Of course, it's possible you may add extra MIDI instruments to the live recording at a later date that you'll have to sync up, but you'll have the luxury of time when you do this. On small-scale productions where there are only two or three instrumentalists in a session (and with the pressures of limited studio time) it's normally safer to record them together.

I once recorded a score for a play that featured clarinet and acoustic guitar. Due to budgets and studio availability, the live room we ended up recording in was very small, although it could comfortably house the two instrumentalists and their music stands. The problem was that they were so close together sound separation became almost impossible. There was a comical moment where the sound engineer and I upended what could only be described as a mattress (although apparently they used it a lot for sound baffling) and trapped it between the floor and the ceiling, in between the two players. We then tied bits of fabric between the mattress and the walls in a vain attempt to cover up any gaps. In reality, this helped very little with the spill; I was never going to be able to separate the instruments from each other. You may ask, why does it matter that there is some sound separation if you're going to use all of the parts in the recording anyway? The cleaner the tracks, the easier to mix the full score at a later date. You'll be able to assign different amounts of compression (and perhaps reverb and other effects) to each track individually. The initial recording often sounds dry and thin: the mixing process is all about making it sound the way you want it to, so it's wise to give yourself the best chance at overall control.

Some larger recording studios have grand or baby grand pianos in them (which sound wonderful), but depending on your budget, you may have to resort to recording MIDI piano. Both have their advantages and drawbacks. Yes, the sound you get from a Steinway or Bösendorfer is unparalleled (although MIDI piano samples now sound incredibly good), but you may have to pay for it to be tuned (which happens by course in a lot of the big studios before every session). MIDI can be altered later, so any mistakes can be ironed out. Sometimes you'll record the audio output of an electric keyboard and not the MIDI so you'll end up having to settle for what your instrumentalist played and the piano sample they used. (It's normally best to record both audio and MIDI from an electronic keyboard at the same time if you can. At least then you have two options to work with.) Audio files from both live and sampled pianos can be processed and experimented with later, so you'll have to make a judgement call on what you think fits best with the aesthetic of the style of music you're recording. In the past when I've recorded complex or classical-sounding piano music, I've tried to record a real piano; classical pianists much prefer the feel of a real piano to a keyboard. If I'm recording a pop tune, an electric piano or keyboard will normally suffice.

Studio Costs

The cost of hiring a studio can vary rather a lot. At time of going to print (May 2016), typical examples of studio costs (in London) are as follows:

- At the upper end of the market, for a large live room capable of recording an orchestra and with sound separation booths (plus senior engineer and assistant engineer):

  Daily rate (12 hours): £2,150 + VAT

  Hourly rate (minimum 3 hours): £185 + £65 set-up + £125 ProTools hire (up to six hours, £250 after that) + VAT
- For a medium/small live room with baby grand piano, capable of recording a small ensemble, plus senior engineer and assistant engineer:

  Daily rate (12 hours): £1,500 + VAT

  Hourly rate (minimum 3 hours): £120 + £125 ProTools hire (up to six hours, £250 after that) + VAT
- At the budget end of the market, for a medium/small live room with baby grand piano (capable of recording a small ensemble, plus junior engineer):

  Daily rate (12 hours): £650 + VAT

  Hourly rate (minimum 3 hours): £120 + VAT

- For a small live room for overdubbing (recording voice work) or at most two instruments (plus junior engineer):
  Daily rate (12 hours): £425 + VAT
  Hourly rate (minimum 3 hours): £100 + VAT

The biggest differences between the most expensive and least expensive studios is in the scale of the studio, the quality of the recording and the aesthetic experience of the session. At the higher end of the market, studios tend to be larger and more comfortable. The more expensive studios have a larger range of equipment so may be able to tailor microphone choice, for example, more specifically for your project. They will also employ the most experienced engineers who come with many years of recording knowledge and will be able to record the best sound quality from your instrumentalists. There's nothing wrong with the cheaper end of the market, you may just have to be a little more hands-on with directing how you want the instruments recorded. It's also worth saying that the 'experience' of the session can sometimes be dictated by the surroundings of the control room (where the engineers mix the music) and the building itself. If you're working for wealthy or important clients sometimes they will be willing to pay more for a nicer and more user-friendly atmosphere in the studio. The high-end studios provide a more opulent experience for the more discerning client and will be able to accommodate larger groups if you so require. When recording for the theatre, you don't usually have that many spectators at a recording session, but in sessions for other media I have known a whole group of executives to sit in the control room. Some of the smaller studios wouldn't be set up for this and it could lead to a bad energy at your session. It's important to understand your parameters from both sides of the control-room glass.

Musicians

Musicians are wonderful creatures. Top-flight professional session players turn up punctually for a recording session, tune up and then record the music with expert precision and artistry, interpreting exactly what is written on the page. They will play it paying full attention to tone and dynamic markings and take on board any notes you have. If adjustments in instrument parameters are required, such as different guitar-pedal sounds, they will be forthcoming with suggestions and work with you to generate the result you're most happy with. If you can work with these people, they will make your life in the recording studio much easier, and for the most part they tend to be generous and respectful – after all, you're the person who's employing them.

Sometimes you'll work with players of a slightly lower calibre, but this doesn't mean your session will be any less productive. Be courteous and respectful towards musicians – they have the ability to lift your music to beautiful places. They are craftsmen and women who spend a large portion of their lives studying and working with their instrument, so they know it inside out. If a piece of fingering or double stopping, for instance, doesn't work, listen to a musician's suggestion and change it to make it work. I remember well the first time I recorded a live harpist in a small orchestral ensemble. The player, unknown to me at the time, is one of the best and most hard-working harpists in the country and yet she took time before the session to go through my scores with me and give any necessary pointers or advice. If you do your homework, you can get a pretty good handle on how to write for any instrument, but there's nothing quite like validation from someone who really knows it intimately. Absorb knowledge from all sources – it will make your work much better in the future.

Booking Musicians

When you've been around for a while and have written and recorded several scores, you will start to get to know musicians personally and will know which ones you particularly like to work with. If you happen to write several scores for the same instrument, there is every chance you'll want to use the same people again and again. Loyalty is important in every aspect of the entertainment business: directors and producers hire you because they like working with you, respect you and trust you to deliver. The same applies to the relationship between composers, conductors and musicians. Most of the time when writing scores for plays, you will have to conduct or 'musically direct' your own recording session. There tends not to be money in the budget to hire external conductors, and because of the interaction in a recording session you can build a rapport with the musicians playing your work. If someone is a very good player and they are pleasant to work with, there's no reason not to employ them again if another suitable job comes along.

Fixers/Orchestral Management Companies

If you don't know a suitable player for your session or you need to book a large number of musicians, the common person to deal with is a 'fixer' (or 'orchestral manager') who can book musicians for recording sessions, concerts and shows. They have a huge list of contacts for players who they send out to all manner of gigs. Fixers also deal with contracts (which saves you the hassle) and often turn up to the session to make sure everything is running smoothly. They are always on the lookout for new musicians to hire and have an astonishingly diverse array of talent on their books. If you need someone who can play an obscure instrument the best person to ask is a fixer. Fixers charge a percentage on top of the session fee per musician, so it is most worth their while when you require a large number of musicians. That's not to say they won't help you if you only need one or two instrumentalists. Fixers understand that relationships in these circles need to be nurtured and as a composer you will hopefully be in a position to hire people again in the future. I have known fixers to do me favours on small jobs because they realise it is in everyone's interest that the work keeps circulating.

Alternatively, you can use the internet to find musicians for your session. A lot of professionals have a diary service that enables you to see their availability and request them for a recording session. The benefit of a fixer is that you know they will have vetted their clients beforehand. If you employ a musician from the internet, even though they have demos you can listen to, there's no way to guarantee they will be useful in a recording studio environment. It is a fixer's job to know who are the best and most appropriate musicians for your session.

Session Fees

When hiring musicians for your session, fees and hours are set by the Musicians' Union (MU). The MU has a collective bargaining agreement for musicians working in the West End of London with the Society of London Theatre (SOLT). It also has House Agreements with companies including the Royal Shakespeare Company, the Royal National Theatre, Regent's Park Open Air Theatre, the Menier Chocolate Factory and Shakespeare's Globe.[52]

Productions outside of London are covered by an agreement with UK Theatre (UKT). For the sake of this section, we'll take the SOLT agreement as an example. If in doubt, contact the MU or relevant society.

Of course, we would all love to pay people more than the minimum for a recording session, but the reality is that a composer's budget is tight in the theatre, and there is unlikely to be a good enough reason to give to a producer as to why they should pay any extra than is necessary. Some gigs pay royalties to musicians and they make up for all the basic rate work. Rates are bound to change in time so make sure to check with the MU before quoting session rates. At the time of printing, the fee structure for non-classical recordings looks like this:[53]

Type of session	Fee	Max. duration	Max. track(s) duration
Standard session	£120	3 hours	20 minutes
Long session	£180	4 hours	30 minutes
Short session	£90	2 hours	10 minutes

For every three-hour session, a break of no less than fifteen minutes must be given. As you can see from the 'Max. Track(s) Duration' column, there is a limit to the amount of music you are eventually allowed to use from any one recording session.

Overdubbing

If you are recording more than one part for the same instrument, it is wise to employ the correct number of musicians rather than ask one to overdub separate lines. The MU guidelines state that an additional fee of 110% of the session fee will be payable to the musician for each overdub recorded. This legislation is put in place to protect musicians' jobs. If you employ more musicians it is better for the industry and cheaper for you.

Doubling and Trebling

If you require a musician to play more than one instrument in a session they are to be paid 25% extra of the session fee for one additional instrument and 40% extra for two additional instruments. For the sake of clarity, tuned mallet instruments, Latin American rhythm instruments, drum kits and timpani are considered one instrument each. If in doubt, check the BPI/MU agreement.[54]

Porterage

The Musicians' Union defines porterage as 'a contribution towards the extra time, effort and additional costs associated with the transportation of large or heavy instruments in order to fulfil an engagement'. Instruments are considered in groups determined by 'whether a large or heavy instrument can reasonably be carried on public transport… or whether it requires transportation by a standard-sized car or larger vehicle'.[55]

As a guide (subject to change):

Group A	*Payment £16.22* Chimes Drums Marimba Vibraphone Xylophone
Group B	*Payment £12.75 (cap £20.50)* Electric accordion Electric guitar Bass saxophone Tuba Double bass

N.B. Limit of payment in Group B for two or more instruments £20.50.

Group C	*Payment £8.22* Contra bassoon Glockenspiel Baritone saxophone Trombone plus 1 other brass instrument or mutes 2 Saxophones Cello
Group D	*Payment to be negotiated between the producer and the performer on a case-by-case basis* Harp Timpani Organ[56]

Other bulky or unusual instruments are considered on an individual basis. If in doubt, check with the MU.

Repeat Fees/Live Backing Track Fees

In addition to the session fee, musicians may be entitled to extra payments for the usage of the recording in a live theatre show. At the National Theatre, for example, instrumentalists whose recording is used in the show are paid an extra £27.63 per performance for up to twenty minutes of music.[57] In the West End (under the agreement with SOLT) if the amount of music (curtain-up, scene change or incidental background) used exceeds four minutes, musicians will also be entitled an extra payment of £7.50 per performance for up to ten minutes' duration, if over ten minutes and up to twenty minutes they receive £1.25 per minute. Consent is required from the MU for any use of recorded music over twenty minutes in length. Consent is also required on a case-by-case basis for interpolated usage/interaction between the music and the performers.[58] These are the gigs that come along every so often for a musician where they can end up making over ten times their original session fee simply from the use of the recording, depending on the length of the show's run.

Existing Groups

Sometimes you may want to record a specific group of instruments that are commonly used together, e.g. a string quartet. In this case, many instrumentalists will already belong to such an ensemble. If you're looking to record a string quartet, you can of course assemble two violinists, a viola player and a cellist, but if you find players that are used to playing in a group together, you can exploit the natural synergy between them for your own benefit. That's not to say that four great players won't gel together, but if an experienced ensemble already exists it can be a shortcut towards better sound balance, integration and short-hand communication between players. This can equally apply to pre-existing bands, jazz ensembles or choral singers.

Preparing for a Session

Once you've composed and arranged all your music, and produced necessary variations on each cue, you'll need to complete the most boring and overlooked part of the job – printing scores. As you become more successful you may find that assistants or producers (normally their assistants) come in useful for this unenviable task. Having said this, I find myself quite frequently opting to do it myself. Printing gives you another chance to check that no obvious mistakes have slipped through the cracks. If you send scores to other people to print, you'll probably have to turn them into PDFs (unless they run the same software as you). You can spend so much time doing this that you might as well have printed them out yourself. Also, in the printing process, I often notice and correct layout peculiarities as I go. Sometimes there is simply too much music or not enough time to do it all on your own, so if you can find someone you trust to do the work either with or for you, then they will be worth their weight in gold. I have been caught out before when parts have gone missing, and it's never something you want to deal with during a recording session when time is of the essence, so double check you have *all* the necessary printing complete.

Printers, Paper and Masking Tape

I would recommend investing in a good laser printer. When you have to print out hundreds of pages of scores before a session, time becomes very precious. Also, use quality paper for your scores. It may seem like an inconsequential thing, but slightly thicker paper sits on music stands much more easily and musicians will thank you for it.

A few words about 'taping'. Taping music is another one of those tasks that you may never have considered existed, but can take hours you may not have budgeted for. One of my very first professional jobs (as an assistant to a musical director) was to print out reams and reams of music for numerous stage shows. A large part of that task was to physically stick all the A4 sheets of a particular piece of music together using masking tape. (Always use masking tape as it can be removed without the paper tearing.) If you are dealing with long medleys this can be quite an extensive job. Make sure you tape the back of the paper and assemble the sheets in a concertinaed manner so they can be opened as would the pages of a book.

Taping music is not completely necessary. I'm sure there are composers out there who have never even considered doing it, but it did teach me about how to relate to musicians and make their lives easier. With big orchestras there tends to be a librarian who looks after all such things, but everything about the process of writing music for plays is a little more homespun. Use your own judgement about whether to tape music for certain instruments. If a piece of music is only two pages long then you won't need to bother. Drummers' parts, if they're quite long, tend to benefit from taping as it makes page turns much easier. Front-line players (i.e. the brass section) don't normally need their music taped, as they typically have more rests and therefore opportunities to manage the music on their stands.

If in doubt, don't tape the music for a recording session, but come armed with a roll of masking tape should anyone need it.

Put all your scores in labelled envelopes for easy distribution to the players.

Recording Session Cue Sheet

Whenever I run a recording session for a play, I like to draw up a document detailing who the instrumentalists are at the session, what instruments they are playing, the name(s) of the recording engineer(s), and the name and order of each cue we need to record. Here is an example from Theatre Royal Bath's West End production of *Hay Fever.*

Case Study: *Hay Fever* in the West End

Composer: Michael Bruce
Clarinet: Ben Woodgate
Guitar: Bryan Smith
Engineer: Marta Salogni

Hay Fever Opening V1 – 110 bpm (rit at bar 8)
Hay Fever Opening V2 – 110 bpm (rit at bar 7,2)
Hay Fever Opening V4 – 110 bpm (rit at bar 7,2)
Hay Fever Opening V3 – 160 bpm (rit at bar 11)
Hay Fever Opening V3.1 – 160 bpm (rit at bar 11)
Hay Fever Opening V5 – 150 bpm (rit at bar 9)
Hay Fever Opening V5.1 – 150 bpm (rit at bar 11)

Hay Fever End of Act 1 V1 – No click
Hay Fever End of Act 1 V2 – No click
Hay Fever End of Act 1 V3 – No click
Hay Fever End of Act 1 V4 – No click
Hay Fever End of Act 1 V5 – No click

Hay Fever Act 2 V1 – 125 bpm
Hay Fever Act 2 V2 – 125 bpm
Hay Fever Act 2 V2.1– 125 bpm
Hay Fever Act 2 V2.2 – 125 bpm
Hay Fever Act 2 V3 – 160 bpm
Hay Fever Act 2 V3.1 – 160 bpm
Hay Fever Act 2 V4 – 150 bpm
Hay Fever Act 2 V4.1 – 150 bpm

Hay Fever Act 3 V1 – 120 bpm (rall at bar 25)
Hay Fever Act 3 V1.1 – 120 bpm (rall at bar 17)
Hay Fever Act 3 V2 – 120 bpm (rit at bar 31)
Hay Fever Act 3 V3 – 160 bpm (rit at bar 43)

Hay Fever Ending – No click
Hay Fever Ending V2 – No click
Hay Fever Ending V3 – No click
Hay Fever Ending V4 – No click
Hay Fever Ending V5 – No click

Hay Fever Bows – 135 bpm

I will include a copy of this cue sheet inside each envelope of parts for every musician and give a copy to the studio engineer alongside a copy of the full scores for the session. It's useful to have a couple of extras lying about the studio in case anyone needs to quickly find out someone's name or where we are in the schedule.

You'll notice that I have also marked the tempos for the click track guide in this document and any moments where tempo changes occur. For this session we recorded to the metronome click in the studio's ProTools session and then muted the click at the free time bars (which were always at the end of a track) where I conducted. If you have an extensive backing track or need a click-track guide with many tempo changes, you should prepare this beforehand. If you are going to prepare tracks you can normally send them to the engineer prior to the session so they can cue them up (or at least provide them first thing). As mentioned before, having sessions recorded to click makes editing and adding MIDI afterwards a lot easier.

Before the Session

The best way to ensure that you have everything you need to run a smooth session is to phone or email your allocated engineer beforehand. Tell them what the project is, what kind of music you'll be recording, which instruments, if you want instruments to be isolated, whether you'll be recording to click, what sample rate you want the session to be recorded at (typically these days 24 bit, 48 kHz) and generally any other information you might think helpful. Good recording studios and engineers will have the live room set up before the start of the session. You should always arrive at least half an hour before the official starting time to check in with the set-up and give the assistant the cue sheet to prepare the ProTools session. If you state that a recording session starts at 10 a.m., it is assumed that that means the red light goes on at 10 a.m. and the recording starts. Musicians should turn up and be ready to play by that time.

It can be a nice touch to hand out sheet music personally to musicians before a session if practical to do so. Use this opportunity to take your scores into the live room and approach each player, introduce yourself and give them the music. In the past I have been in recording sessions where no one has met anyone officially and it can feel a little less conducive to a creative atmosphere, especially when you start giving notes. The cue sheet comes in most helpful here as you can use it to refer to each person by name rather than calling them, for example, 'second trombone'. Of course if you're recording a large ensemble this may not be practical and instrumentalists will forgive you for not knowing their names, but it's common courtesy to at least attempt to do so with a small group of musicians.

The Studio Engineer

Professional recording studios normally allocate you at least one recording engineer to run your session. They will normally be experienced in all kinds of projects. Some remain 'in-house' and only work for a particular studio and some are freelance. When you book a session you can request a specific in-house engineer if you have worked with them previously and get on; otherwise they will allocate you someone they think will suit your project. Most of the time, recording engineers are enthusiastic and generous, and tend to be open-minded or even intrigued by whatever music you might be recording that day.

On one occasion, however, I was lumbered with an 'old rocker' who showed up late to the session, stank of booze, couldn't be less interested in the project, actively disapproved of the client (it was an advert), and didn't do a very good job of recording or mixing the track. Safe to say, I've never returned to that studio again, which is a pity because I'm sure there are others who work there who would have done a perfectly good job.

Bigger studios tend to have very experienced engineers who work with an assistant. With this set-up, the engineer is concerned with the sound and quality of the recording (sits at the mixing desk), and works with you (the client) to achieve the results you are after. If you are in the live room conducting, they will be able to tell you when a take sounds particularly good or if there are any recording errors. Otherwise you can sit with them in the control room and listen together. I find good studio engineers are an invaluable extra, objective pair of ears to have during a recording session. Meanwhile, the assistant will be running the ProTools session, recording and labelling takes.

In this instance the assistant will also make a 'Take Sheet' marking notes on various takes of cues so that you can later reference which were particularly good. There's an example below.

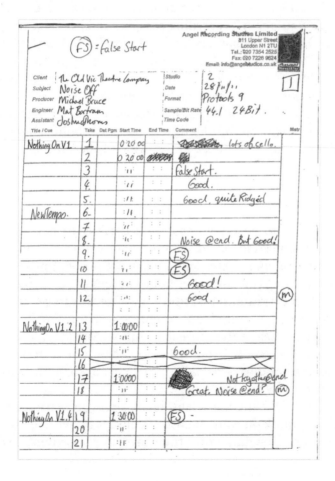

(FS) = False Start

Angel Recording Studios Limited
311 Upper Street
London N1 2TU
Tel.: 020 7354 2525
Fax: 020 7226 9624
Email: info@angelstudios.co.uk

Client: The Old Vic Theatre Company
Subject: Noise Off
Producer: Michael Bruce
Engineer: Mat Bartram
Assistant: Joshua Thomas

Studio: 2
Date: 28/../..
Format: Protools 9
Sample/Bit Rate: 44.1 24Bit.
Time Code:

Title / Cue	Take	Dat Pgm	Start Time	End Time	Comment	Mstr
Nothing On V1	1		0:20:00	: :	lots of cello.	
	2		0:20:00			
	3		"	: :	False Start.	
	4.		"	: :	Good.	
	5.		"	: :	Good, quite Ridged	
New Tempo.	6.		"	: :		
	7		"	: :		
	8.		"	: :	Noise @end. But Good!	
	9.		"	: :	(FS)	
	10		"	: :	(FS)	
	11		"	: :	Good!	
	12.		"	: :	Good..	(m)
			: :	: :		
Nothing On V1.2	13		1:00:00	: :		
	14		"	: :		
	15		"	: :	Good.	
	16					
	17		1:00:00	: :	Not together @end.	
	18		"	: :	Great. Noise @end?	(m)
			: :	: :		
Nothing On V1.4	19		1:30:00	: :	(FS) -	
	20		"	: :		
	21		"	: :		

The studio engineer can also help you mix your music (if required). Sometimes with a score for a play you'll want to mix at home and add extra MIDI instruments, etc. If this is the case you'll need to take away either the ProTools session files (if you run ProTools at home) or get the assistant to create audio 'stems'. Stems are audio files of separate instrument channels on each take. They can be individual instrument channels or groups of similar instruments. You can then import these into whatever software program you choose. To export stems takes a little extra time at the end of a session so you should budget your time accordingly if you know this is what you need. These days you can also normally source all the audio files from the original ProTools audio folders which saves time doing separate exports. Before you begin a recording session, make it clear to the studio engineer what it is you want to walk away with at the end of the session and check how best to achieve that. It's a good idea to invest in a portable hard drive with a FireWire connection (or whatever the latest and fastest data cable is) to take to all your sessions. Alternatively, the engineer may wish to upload all the files to a shared folder online, but this will take longer to upload and download at each end.

Running the Session

Make sure to pace your session according to how much music you need to record and how much extra time you may need for mixing or stemming parts at the end. Musicians' sessions are typically three hours in length so if you can afford an extra hour of studio time after this to get all the necessary files compiled it might be worth it. You'll then make the most of the musicians' time. Overtime for musicians is incredibly expensive so it's best not to run over schedule. Studios also charge overtime, but sometimes that is a necessary burden to bear.

Try to take the musicians' break after you've passed the halfway mark on your cue list. It's always better to go back to less and hopefully you'll then have the opportunity to do any additional retakes at the end. Usually by the mid-point of the session if the music is all of a similar style, musicians will get on a roll and rattle through the various cues. Occasionally, though, you may be forced to make a judgement call and choose not to record certain cues that you think are least likely to be useful. Sometimes you will hear a cue and realise that it isn't appropriate, so you might as well not record any of its other variations.

Running a recording session is a bit like directing a play in that you have to understand when and how to give notes. I have heard it said that in a rehearsal room, 80% of the people know when something isn't working properly, 60% know what the note should be, but only 10% know *when* and *how* to give the note. This person is the director. A large part of directing is about relationships and people management: so is running a studio session, but with a much shorter timescale.

Working with children requires a slightly gentler approach. (Mostly I've come across this with child singers.) It sounds obvious, but because a child's attention span is shorter, you need to work out how best to break up the session so that you get all that you need without piling on any unnecessary pressure.

Case Study: Accidents

I am sure that one of the recording engineer's worst nightmares is that they don't record a cue properly when they think they have. This once happened to me on a project that required a lot of music to be recorded in one session by an ensemble of three. After listening back to the first few takes we were so happy we rattled through the rest of the session without making time to listen back as we went. It wasn't until I got the audio files to my home computer that I realised the engineer had gone on to make an error with the 'pre-roll' (the delay between the click starting and the processor actually recording the music) at the start of all the subsequent tracks. This meant the first bar of each take hadn't been recorded; rendering most of the audio files unusable in their current form. Needless to say, this felt like a complete disaster.

At the time I was juggling two shows in different parts of the country and had no time to re-record any music. I'm sure that the studio engineer in question has never forgotten the phone call that followed my realisation of the extent of the catastrophe, but unfortunately there was nothing that could be done. It was too late in the process to record any more music, I was in a different part of the country to the studio, and the instrumentalists (who were very specialised) were no longer available. This meant I had to improvise with some incredibly creative editing and add a great deal of MIDI instrumentation to cover up the fact that the upbeats to most of the tracks were missing. In the end, I managed to make it work, but it was an extra level of stress that was rather unwelcome. In hindsight, I should probably have insisted we listen through the tracks as we went, but in reality this wasn't possible due to time constraints. I am sure that this was a freak one-off accident and I'd be willing to put money on the fact that that engineer will never let it happen again, but sometimes disasters happen – the important thing is not to lose your head but come up with a practical solution.

Writing music is not a life or death way to make a living, but it can be incredibly frustrating when unexpected things go wrong. Rest assured though, things will go wrong – a lot – so you must make sure you are prepared to cope when they do.

Case Study: Musician Meltdown

Most of the time, professional musicians are accustomed to taking direction and notes, and will correct themselves without any animosity towards the conductor or musical director. Occasionally, though, you may come across a musician who is not accustomed to the recording environment and will tense up when the red light goes on. I once worked with a jazz player who found it very tricky to play in small bursts for individual cues and remain in tune. I realised (too late) that he was used to playing live jazz gigs where the musical structure tends to be freer and focused on the long line of melodic improvisation. The main goals there are the feel of the music and creativity, and there's time to build up to a piece of improvisation.

The repetitive nature of recording various takes of similar cues was alien to him and unfortunately he lost his intonation and his bottle. In this situation you have to deal with what you've got, and what I had was a very good live instrumentalist struggling with the pressurised nature of recording. The only thing to do is to try and release that pressure – be supportive and adjust your expectations in terms of the amount of music and adapt your cue list to include only the most likely candidates for incorporation in the final show. In this case I recorded some of the longer cues first so that he had space to get used to the nature of how his improvisations could work in tandem with the rest of the score. It's worth noting that even the best players can have off days. It is your job to get the most out of them in whatever time you have.

Conducting

Some composers like conducting their own work, some don't. Personally I enjoy conducting, but only when necessary. It depends very much on the style of music. If I'm recording very short cues to click, I prefer to sit in the control room with the engineer so I can hear the recorded sound, rather than the acoustic sound in the live room. This gives a clearer indication of how the eventual track will turn out. I can then give precise notes to musicians in between takes, but don't need to be in the room waving a baton in their faces. If I'm recording something with a large ensemble and without click then I'm likely to want to conduct, but trying to conduct something like pop or rock music is often unnecessary. It's all about understanding the requirements of the score.

In general, cues for plays tend to be quite short so the recording process can be a little fragmented. Conducting can be vital to get the best performance out of an ensemble of musicians, but if you're recording ten-second bursts of scene-change music to click, the notes you give between takes will be as useful as the physical act of conducting during them. I love conducting, but if it's unneeded or even unhelpful it's best to be realistic, acknowledge that and step out of the way.

Backing Tracks

If you've created a backing track for your instrumentalists to play along to, and there are lots of tempo changes, you will want to make sure that you have recorded a synced click track to go along with it. If you're running ProTools then it's possible that you can share the session file with the engineer and record directly onto it. If, however, you run a different type of software, the best thing to do is to stem your backing track and click track as two separate audio files. This means that when they're played together in the studio session, the engineer will have control over the click and track volumes separately. Musicians always ask for different levels of click and track so it's best to be prepared. If, however, the music remains in one tempo throughout you'll be able to sync it up with the metronome in ProTools and won't require an additional exported click track.

Comping

Comping (or 'compiling') is the process by which you edit various takes of the same instrument line together to produce the optimum performance. Historically this was done by cutting ('splicing') the tape with a razor blade and sticking the best bits of the reel back together. In the modern studio, comping is done digitally, so engineers can sometimes do it in stages as you go along. Even a rough 'placeholder' comp of two takes can come in useful to use as a backing for some other instrumental or vocal overdubs later on.

Sometimes an instrumentalist will want to 'punch in', which means picking up the recording of a cue from a midpoint (usually just before they made an error). This new section will then be grafted onto the good part of the previous take in the comping process. A lot of the time you end up doing your comping at home when you mix the show versions of your tracks. You can use your 'take sheet' as a reference to find the best moments and combine them together.

Comping forms a large part of mixing vocal tracks and can even be used to cut and splice individual breath-noises and notes to create a performance that never happened. Auto-tune is also frequently used while mixing vocals and as a producer once told me: 'Almost everything released these days has been auto-tuned – if you don't auto-tune even a perfectly good vocal it will sound under par when compared to those that have been. So we auto-tune everything.' How depressing.

Mixing

Engineers come into their own when mixing tracks. If an assistant has been running the ProTools session, after the musicians have gone, the engineer will take over the reins and start to mix, compress, add reverb, EQ and various effects. Depending on your circumstances, you may not need the engineer to mix tracks for you; it's possible to do it all at home. When we recorded the album of *Much Ado About Nothing*, we were given a week in the recording studio totalling two days (four sessions) with the musicians, a day with the vocalists and two days worth of mixing. This was such a big project that it made sense to do all the mixing in the recording studio. Smaller plays tend not to need this amount of technical support.

It's also worth noting that even after you've mixed your tracks on headphones, home speakers or in a professional recording studio, you will inevitably want to do some remixing when you hear them played through the theatre speaker system. If you have mixed it yourself at home this is not a huge problem as you can redo it in the theatre space. If your music is to be fully mixed in the recording studio, it's advisable to take away stems of various instrument groupings afterwards. You can then reassemble them on your own computer and adjust. Sometimes you may even want to give individual stems to the sound designer and mix the music directly through the theatre system. (More on this in the section on working with sound designers.)

Visitors in the Recording Studio

Sometimes sound designers will come along to your recording session to get a feel for the music you're going to provide for the show. If you have a close working relationship with a sound designer he can often provide inspiration or ideas during the recording process that will link in with the sound design. Most of the time, however, they don't need to be there and they tend to be very busy towards the end of the rehearsal process anyway.

It's very uncommon for a director or producer to want to come to the recording studio, but I have known it to happen on occasion. Be very careful to make them aware that the sound they hear in the studio is a work in progress and will not sound the same after it has been mixed. Often a director just wants to get an early preview of the recorded music, so it's usually best that they come in near the end of the session. You enter very murky waters if a director starts trying to give direction during a recording. You need to assume the role of the leader with the clear vision in these sessions. Having a director give notes in the middle of a recording session is highly inadvisable. That way madness lies.

I have spent some of my happiest career moments in recording studios listening to my music being played. If you surround yourself with highly skilled, hard-working and friendly people, and helm a focused but joyous ship, the sound of the resulting recording will benefit greatly. Time in the recording studio is expensive and precious so the best piece of advice I could give is to make sure you come as prepared as possible. Then you stand the best chance of leaving with all the music you came for and perhaps even something special inspired in the moment.

Performing Live

Why Live Music?

You may well ask, especially when we've spent so much time looking at the recorded score. Music, at its heart is a live medium and has become slightly overlooked in recent times with regards to its importance to the play (hence part of the reason for this book). Recorded music is incredibly good at setting tone, mood or for driving narrative, but there is a magical quality, something unquantifiable about the energy that you get from a live music performance that you don't get on a recording.

This might be partly to do with the fact that it is, in fact, live, as in never to be repeated in exactly the same way again, much in the same way that every acting performance in the theatre is a one-off. Once each note is played, or each line of dialogue is spoken, it's gone forever.

When people talk about the joy of live music they frequently cite the idea that the physical act of seeing musicians play enriches their experience (which is a good reason to be able to see your live band rather than hide them away, providing they don't become an unwanted distraction). The charged energy that's created between audience and performer is a vital part of why live theatre works, whether that performer is an actor, a musician or both.

Live musicians also feed off each other's energy and the energy of the acting company and this enhances the storytelling. Musicians who are part of the production – who get to see it and play for it every night – will be able to form a much better understanding of how the music functions as a part of the show. You open the 'circle of collaboration' even wider, providing more scope for detailed interpretation (which a musical director will maintain and control) from a larger group of skilled individuals. Tiny adjustments in a band's performance as their work matures alongside the acting company and the production as a whole will keep the energy and thrill of the play alive. Depending on the style of music and its function in the production you may find that a recorded score is preferable, but if you have the opportunity to use a live band, and it fits with the premise of the show, then you will not regret it.

The composition and production process when using a live band is slightly different to that of a recorded score, which is what we'll be examining here. There are two ways of incorporating live music into a play: through actor-musicians (onstage); or a dedicated band of non-acting musicians in a pit, band room or platform, on or attached to the playing area. We'll begin by looking at these non-acting musicians and the process of working with them.

Choosing Your Line-up

If you're lucky enough to be granted the use of a live band for your production you will, of course, be working within a tight budget. As it's so expensive, you tend not to be working with huge ensembles, but it's amazing what you can achieve with a relatively small number of live instruments.

The RSC regularly works with live bands in their two main spaces: in the smaller Swan Theatre there is typically a band of seven and in the larger Royal Shakespeare Theatre this expands to the luxury of eight. These both include a musical director as one of their number who will usually play keyboards and sometimes double up on other instruments. Altogether you're looking at half a dozen or so instruments to create your musical world.

At the time of writing, the RSC are also unique in that they have a house band on permanent contract with the company. The allocation of these players is spread across the two theatres meaning there are certain instruments that you will be required to incorporate into your score. You then top up the remaining chairs in your ensemble with what are deemed 'pro rata' musicians of your choice, who must live within a commutable distance. It sounds complicated but it isn't. The only drawback is that you may end up with an instrument line-up that is slightly off-kilter with your ideal choice. I always stand by the idea (it certainly applies to me) that if you give creative people limits within which to work, it forces them to be their most creative and come up with solutions. A blank cheque can be a curse for creativity.

Sometimes, however, due to necessary musical styles, a live line-up can be tricky to make work. With a pre-recorded score you have the capacity to do a lot with MIDI sequencers and samples, so you can top up any live instrumentation with computer-generated sounds. You can also do this (within reason) with a live band by either using keyboards to trigger samples or by recording them and playing along to a click track. In my opinion, when using live music in a play, everything that can be played live should be played live: there's not a lot of good in having a band of live musicians sit still while you play pre-recorded music. That's not in the spirit of the venture.

Case Study: *Candide* for the Royal Shakespeare Company

It's always your job as a composer to try to find a way to make anything possible musically. When I scored Mark Ravenhill's response to Voltaire's *Candide*, there were to be five different locations with five different sound worlds, four of which were to be musicalised. Breaking them down scene by scene: the first was in the style of an eighteenth-century operetta and required instruments that could support that; the second was set in the present day at an eighteenth birthday party with a function band; the third was set in a film executive's office and required sound design rather than music; the fourth was set in El Dorado, hundreds of years ago, and required a South American folk vibe; and the fifth was set in the future at an experimental scientific and medical institute – it needed to sound futuristic and (for want of a better word) 'alien'.

Achieving all of these very different sound worlds was difficult with seven instruments, but it presented an opportunity for clever instrumentation. We achieved all we needed with keyboards, violin, cello, guitar (acoustic and electric), trumpet, bass (upright and electric) and percussion (various instruments including timpani, congas, cymbals and drum kit). Thankfully, instrumentalists are permitted (within reason) to double up on various instruments if necessary and are financially compensated by the RSC. You should always check with your producer about doubling of instruments as it inflates costs. The acoustic instruments, violin, cello, upright bass, timpani and trumpet, along with piano or harpsichord samples on keyboards, created a sustainable musical palette for the operetta section; the electric guitar and bass along with the drum kit, strings and keyboards provided our function-band sound; the acoustic guitar, strings and various percussion (including other band members providing hand-claps) gave us the feel for El Dorado; and the final scene was a rather unusual combination of click track (featuring sound effects edited into musical phrases) accompanied by the entire band 'playing' a variety of medical equipment through microphones. This was as bonkers as it sounds, but it gave a very unique feel (and look) to the final scene. It is to the credit of the musicians involved and the spirit of 'inclusivity of music' at the RSC that these top-quality musicians played rhythmic variations on a bed pan and blown-up rubber glove and made it work.

Sound-department Requirements

You normally have to decide your instrument line-up very early in the process. This is purely logistical from the standpoint of musicians' availability and sound-department requirements, but can happen so early on that you inevitably just have to take your best guess at what your needs will be. It's not uncommon to be getting emails about your line-up weeks before rehearsals start. The sound department have to make sure they have the necessary equipment to support whatever line-up you choose. They too have their own budgetary restrictions, so it may be that you have to compromise on certain instrument selections: their size, for example, can be a problem if space is limited. They also need to know if players are doubling on instruments so they can be properly mic'd and whether there are enough microphones to go around (if, for example, you also require onstage singers to be amplified).

It's worth saying that sound departments are usually brilliant at helping you to achieve the sound you desire. They will go out of their way to make the impossible possible, but compromises will inevitably have to be made. The sound designer will also work in tandem with the sound department to deliver the overall production sound, so between all of you, you should be able to come up with creative and workable solutions for each eventuality.

Auditioning

Of course, as well as giving sound specifications early in the process you will also have to book your instrumentalists. Music departments by their very nature tend to be well equipped to find you appropriate players to consider. They often have standing relationships with players they know will deliver, but if they are looking for someone new to the company they will likely ask them to audition. You should attend auditions if possible. It sounds obvious, but it's good practice to hear people play before you hire them, which, of course, doesn't happen when you fix a recording session through a fixer. Likewise, sometimes you have to trust your music department to find players with the appropriate abilities.

If you do audition people, it is common courtesy to give them an idea of the style of music in the show. At this stage you normally won't have written any of it yet, so you need to be able to give a general guideline summary of the score you plan to write. It is normal practice for a player to prepare two contrasting pieces of music within the boundaries of the style you've suggested. (If there are going to be many contrasting styles you may need to ask them to prepare more.) In this audition you should be looking at whether they are technically able to deliver the kind of music you plan to write; if they can fulfil any extra necessary requirements such as improvisation; how open they are to the process, knowing that these requirements may change before the final show; and crucially whether or not you feel they will bring the necessary spirit to the production – in their performance and their willingness to join in with the rest of the band and company. Sometimes live musicians will be required to wear a costume and appear on stage, so you need to make sure that any prospective musicians are aware of (and okay with) this before you hire them.

Your musical director will also be a crucial part of auditions. They will be working directly with the band long after you are gone so their opinion is paramount. They will also have lots of experience of playing with pit musicians so they will know what to look out for. Listen and absorb the knowledge and opinions of those around you. Everyone wants to find the best person for the job.

Working with a Musical Director

The musical director (MD) is the person you will have the most regular contact with during the rehearsal process, and along with the sound designer the most contact during the technical rehearsal. A musical director will teach music to the cast and play for rehearsals. When I worked on the opening operetta-style act for *Candide* it was very useful to have the MD in the rehearsal room to play the piano as a guide for the actors. The music ran underneath almost the entirety of the thirty-minute scene and added a lot in terms of narrative function, so it was vital that the actors had a version to rehearse to. Musical directors will spend time with the cast, coaching and rehearsing with singers, or working on instrument technique with anyone who is required to play as part of the show. They will also schedule and run the band call(s), which is the first opportunity you get to hear your score played in full by the instrumentalists. As with a recorded score, I usually find this the most thrilling part of any process.

The Band Call and Sitzprobe

If the band are not members of the cast (i.e. actor-musicians) the band call will usually happen somewhere during the last week of the rehearsal period.

You prepare parts for this call in the same way you would for a recording session, but you tend not to need to prepare as many variations on the same cue as you would for a recorded score. One of the many advantages of live musicians is that you're able to give notes as you go along, or you can try new ideas out in the band call or technical rehearsal, sometimes without even having to write anything down. This rehearsal is a good opportunity to make notes on anything that maybe doesn't quite work musically or that you simply don't like. You don't have to go into the band call thinking your score is complete. The beauty of holding this session the week before technical rehearsals start is that you can keep things fluid (to a certain degree). Try to get every cue working as well as possible and if necessary suggest a few cuts or edits to the parts as you go along, but bear in mind that this is also an opportunity for the musicians to get their heads around the music and flag up any problem areas. They will be sight-reading at this rehearsal so may choose to take certain passages away to practise if needs be.

It can be daunting having musicians scrutinise your work in a band call, but know that they are only trying to do their jobs to the best of their ability. If people ask questions about moments in your writing it is normally because they are seeking clarity. Try not to feel as if they are judging you. This is a two-way street – many musicians get nervous having to sight-read scores in front of the person who wrote them, especially in small ensembles. Try to alleviate any tension or stress by being personable and open, and don't judge musicians based on their ability to sight-read. Most of them sight-read very well, but will improve a good deal even by the next pass.

If the score requires the cast to interact with the music (usually singing) you'll have what is known as a Sitzprobe (seated rehearsal). The term originally comes from opera where singers sat on stage as they ran through the music together with the orchestra (in the pit) for the first time.

Case Study: *The Two Gentlemen of Verona* for the Royal Shakespeare Company

Occasionally, you may want members of your band to appear on stage as part of a scene. In the RSC's production of *The Two Gentlemen of Verona* we had four of our eight-piece band appear on stage as members of the company to play the song 'Who is Silvia?'. The most important of these was the guitarist whose part was the foundation for the whole number. He had to play in sync with one of the actors (who was also playing guitar) and accompany another who was singing the song, so he attended acting company rehearsals for this moment as much as possible. This helped to soften the shock for the company when they were suddenly accompanied by three more musicians on stage and four others on the band platform.

Sometimes, a director will deem it necessary to run the play with the whole band in the rehearsal room. This can be incredibly useful and happened with *Candide*. There was so much action and dialogue that had to sync with music, that without this additional call, getting the show together in the technical rehearsal would have been incredibly difficult. This is also an added opportunity for the cast and creative team to get a sense of how the music will function in its full form as part of the production.

It is good practice to remember how fortunate you, the cast, the director and the musicians themselves are to be working on a show that uses live music. Have fun with your band. Allow them feel a part of the creative process – listen to their ideas, and absorb their instrumental knowledge. Treat them with respect and not only will your score end up sounding better, you will make the most of your time working with them on it.

Deps

A dep (short for 'deputy') is a stand-in for a musician when they're ill (or have a better paid gig...). They are very common in all aspects of the live-music world and as they don't have the same amount of rehearsal (if any at all) they often have to be even more accomplished musicians than the regulars they replace. At the beginning of most contracts, the regular band members will nominate their deps and get them validated by the musical director and music department. Different players will produce different sound levels, so the sound engineer will have to pay extra close attention to the mix on a performance that is 'depped out'. Deps will often 'sit in' on a performance so they can study the score and requirements of the player they are going to fill in for. Sometimes the sound of a different player will bring a new freshness to a score (or indeed make it sound worse), but in any case, it is an impressive feat to play a show with no real rehearsal. There are musicians who make their living by only depping and never taking over a 'chair' permanently.

Working with Live Click Tracks

When I was starting out, in the days before everything was run on computers, click tracks were recorded onto minidisks, as they were seen to be the most stable format. One of my first jobs was on a cruise ship as a musical director of production shows, which were comprised mostly of all-singing, all-dancing medleys of show tunes, jazz standards and light-entertainment music. My job was unusual because the ship had a separate musical director on board who performed the shows whilst I taught the shows, addressed the sound balance in the auditorium and kept an eye on the acting company performances. Occasionally I would get the chance to play a show as well which was always fun. The ship bands consisted of seven players who played to a click track featuring extra instrumentation, strings, sound effects and tracked backing vocals. We had seventeen, hour-long shows to perform as part of our contract (which seems like a mad amount even now) and I used to wonder at the reliability of the click tracks. These would comprise quite a large part of the music for every show and were recorded on a little disk that was ferried around from port to port. I used to wonder why they never went wrong.

The truth is, they did go wrong... a lot. I remember one medley in particular, which featured 'ghost vocals' for singers who couldn't quite reach the high notes at the end. It featured a famous song (from a musical with masks and chandeliers) in which the last few moments of the medley consisted of a series of exceptionally high soprano notes unsupported by any other instrumentation. The sound operator would typically fade up the backing track with the pre-recorded voice towards the end of the number. Imagine the horror that crept across my face one day when from the back of the auditorium I realised the track had gone down and there was no way to warn the singer. Two minutes later she was silently opening and shutting her mouth like a fish while the audience looked on in bewilderment.

These days, at least in the UK, theatre click tracks are usually run from a computer program called QLab. This is one of the most stable ways to run music as part of a show and if something goes wrong, there is a back-up machine running alongside it.

One thing that hasn't changed with click tracks is the necessity for there to be audio count-ins on any introductions or significant tempo changes. The way a click track works in a theatre is that you split the audio track and the metronome track onto separate channels. Play them together and the band can play along to just the click or can have a mix of track and click. The audience obviously only hear the track part mixed with the live music. The metronome marks time, but when you are looking to change to a new tempo (as part of a medley, for instance) you should record a vocal count over the first bar in the new tempo and combine it with the metronome track. This helps musicians adjust to the new tempo. When clicks suddenly change tempo without an audio count, go wrong, or are out of sync with the score, it can be next to impossible to work out where you are. Many a car-crash in a band call has happened because someone miscounted bars somewhere and a new tempo began without warning.

Sound-department Roles

The sound department includes various technical staff that will fit and maintain the sound equipment in the theatre for the duration of the run. The members of this team you are most likely to have direct contact with are the 'sound numbers one and two'. The 'sound number one' is normally the sound operator (or mixing engineer) who will mix the show on a nightly basis. The 'sound number two' is typically the person who helps keep the sound equipment in the building functioning, monitors the paperwork, checks the sound system on a daily basis (which involves playing music through every speaker individually to make sure they're all working), maintains musicians' microphone placement and upkeep, and checks and fits microphones to actors.

The sound department will also deal with the technical set-up of cue lights, talk-back systems and 'cans'. Cans is the colloquial term for theatre headsets which combine an earpiece and microphone and are used for communication between departments.

Sound Checks

Before the technical rehearsal begins you will have a 'seating call' and 'sound check' in the theatre with the band in situ. This will happen sometime after your band call (which may have been the previous week) and will typically last for three hours (which is one regular session slot for a musician). The seating call is about getting the band in the optimum position for their comfort and addressing the practicality of any entrances and exits they may need to make from the band area. It's also about finding the correct positions for music stands and microphones. The musical director will normally be playing as part of the band so at this point you will start working most closely with the sound designer.

A 'line check' makes sure all microphones and connections are working properly. After this, each individual instrument will be sound checked and levels will be set for reverb, compression and EQ. The band will then start playing through each cue and the sound designer and sound operator will set volume levels and balance the overall sound. It's best to allow these people to do their jobs and only pitch in when necessary. Most sound designers will ask your opinion as they go along. Although you may not be all that technically minded when it comes to sound design, trust your ears and pass on any useful ideas even if you don't necessarily know how to action them. If you can describe well what it is you think isn't working, then a good sound designer or operator can work out how to solve it and work with you to do so.

Line of Communication

When you're working with a recorded score and the director gives you a note on a music cue during a technical rehearsal, it is a straightforward process to edit your music, incorporate the note and pass it to the sound designer who will cue it up. Depending on what changes have to be made (and whether or not it will affect other people) you may be able to do this very quickly and in real time. Otherwise, use common sense: avoid holding up the tech unnecessarily, take it as a note and do the edit later. When you're working with a live band this becomes a little more complex. Sometimes directors who are accustomed to working only with the composer and sound designer in a technical rehearsal find the process a little disconcerting because the chain of communication is much longer. Even if only a small change is requested, you may need to tell the sound designer, you will definitely have to tell the sound operator and the musical director, who will then have to pass it on the musicians, who may in turn have a question about the note, in which case it has to come back through the musical director to you, and then possibly to the director again. In a good working environment where everyone is tuned into each other, this doesn't take very long. In the midst of a challenging or anxiety-ridden tech, these extra precious seconds can create tension between departments. Also, because there are so many more people involved, the margin for human error is greater: even if you've given the note and you think it's very clear and has been understood, between the player, the MD, the sound designer and the sound operator something may go wrong – and the director will turn to you to correct it. When you're working with a recorded score, you can be completely in charge of what the audience will hear. With a live band no single cue is ever quite the same twice in a row, which is part of what makes it so special. Working with live musicians, you have to learn to relinquish a certain amount of control.

If you have to significantly change or even replace a music cue in tech, you will have to work very quickly to avoid holding the whole process up. Because of this I would recommend, if at all possible, having a printer on your production desk. I have often written new scores during a tech, printed them off and run them up to the band whilst the tech is in session. If you are able to work very quickly then this is an option, but make sure it's a realistic one. There are usually lots of people waiting for the new cue so that the rehearsal can continue, and the pressure to get it done and get it right can become pretty high. However, there is something quite magical about writing a cue one minute and having a whole band play it to an expectant group the next (and it being a success).

Even if you are only making tiny changes to scores that players can mark up themselves, it is usually good practice to reprint their scores with the proper markings included. Sometimes at the end of a preview process, the musical director will take the program files of all the original scores and reprint them with a clearer layout. This just makes them more presentable, easier for deps to read, and better for the archivist to store.

Recording Albums

Very rarely, a theatre company or producer may wish to release an album of the score you've written for a play. When this happens it is in the best interests of the producer to release the album as soon as the play has officially opened. In order to get the CD pressed and ready for sale, you may have to record it long before the technical rehearsal. I once recorded an album of the score for a play a few weeks before the show was fully formed. Inevitably I wrote and recorded some music that then didn't end up in the play. These albums are intended to give more of a flavour of a production rather than be the exact versions of cues that are featured. Because of this, and because you'll want to make it an album worth listening to, you may also have to extend cues beyond the scope of what you intend to be in the show. If it's a live score and you're lucky, you'll get to hold a band call for the purposes of the recording, which essentially gives you an extra rehearsal with the musicians.

If you are given the opportunity to release the score for a play, you should grab it with both hands. The very nature of theatre work is that it's transitory so if you can release a recording for posterity then that's a lovely added bonus.

Maintaining Relationships

The theatre industry is an incredibly small one and the musicians who frequent it are an even rarer breed. As a composer in the theatre it's likely that you will come across or want to use the same people again and again. During the technical and preview periods, try to get to know your band – have a cup of tea with them in a break or take them out for a drink after a performance. Alongside the musical director it's important that you try to run a happy ship.

Working with a live band is a privilege; you should endeavour to make it an enjoyable experience for all.

Working with Actor-Musicians

In the mid-2000s, actor-musicians were thrown into the limelight because of the mainstream success of John Doyle's actor-musician versions of Sondheim's *Sweeney Todd* and *Company*. Doyle's approach dispensed with the typical large orchestra and asked the actors not only to perform their roles but also to play the music themselves live on stage. As Lyn Gardner's article in the *Guardian* in 2008 attested: 'No sooner had Patti Lupone's Mrs Lovett been serenading the grisly delights of her unwholesome pies [in *Sweeney Todd*] than she was blowing a tuba.'[59]

Actor-musicians were nothing new at this point. Financial constraints during the 1980s and '90s meant that regional theatres had to become creative with how they staged their musicals. There was no money for orchestras, so the casts would have to play for themselves – this led to a new kind of creative staging that helped to breathe fresh life into classic pieces.[60] As Gardner asserts: 'In his productions of shows such as *Cabaret* and *Fiddler on the Roof*, Doyle discovered that having the actors play the instruments on stage created a compelling psychological dance, one that both heightened and illuminated the drama.'[61]

Even more recently, the Broadway and West End hit musical *Once* incorporated the use of actor-musicians into the framework of its plot. Audiences love to see multi-talented performers sing, act, dance and play instruments on stage. There is a certain amount of fascination surrounding great actor-musicians, and this section will try to further unlock that and look at the process of working with them in more detail.

A Breed Apart

Good actor-musicians need to be incredibly versatile and multi-talented to be successful in their roles. There are now dedicated courses at drama colleges that work exclusively on the process of becoming an actor-musician. In an ideal world they need to be as good an actor as any non-playing professional actor would be, and they need to be as good a musician as any professional musician. This is a difficult combination to achieve and thus there are not a huge number of performers who legitimately span both areas well. When you do find them they are invaluable.

Actor-Musicians in Plays

As this book focuses on plays let us examine in which circumstances you might come across the need for an actor-musician there. The most likely scenario is that your play incorporates a featured song that requires a singer or instrumentalist (or combination of both).

You may be looking for an actor-musician who has to do more than sing a song in the play. In the Lyric Hammersmith stage adaptation of Sarah Waters' novel *Tipping the Velvet*, the five actor-musicians (plus MD) provided the entire score for the show and played numerous instruments and characters throughout. To tackle some roles, an actor-musician has to sustain a whole evening's worth of acting and playing. If this is the case you want to make sure you're hiring someone with the appropriate level of experience, technique and stamina.

Casting

Finding an actor-musician with the right combination of instrument, acting ability and appearance is a very difficult process, and you are likely to audition lots of people before you find the right fit. You should keep in mind that because actor-musicians are all very individual in their instrument choices, you might have to limit your expectations and adjust your requirements around the performers you cast. Sometimes there simply might not be anyone with the right combination of qualities you were ideally looking for.

If you're auditioning someone for a featured singer role, you will typically ask him or her to bring one or two songs with them (just as you would with musicians). Depending on the style of your production, try to give them as much of a heads-up as to what sort of song you might be looking for before they come to the audition. If they're preparing two songs they should be contrasting within the style of the piece. Sometimes you may even want to send them a specific score to look at. They will be expected to perform with your audition pianist or will sometimes accompany themselves. You will always come across one or two performers who arrive without sheet music and ask to sing a capella. Whilst this is okay, I'd suggest that before you cast anyone you should hear them sing along with an external accompaniment of some sort (i.e. one they are not playing themselves), preferably with a song you have suggested. I was once caught out by a performer who auditioned with a very good rendition of a song on which he accompanied himself, and only after he was cast did I discover that this was the only song he could play and he'd been playing it at auditions for over twenty years.

Auditions are difficult for performers at the best of times and for actor-musicians there is the added anxiety of playing an instrument and singing, as well as reading text. Because of this, you should try even harder to make them feel as at ease as possible and allow extra time per audition slot for instrument set-up. There is a big cultural difference between auditioning for musicals and plays. In musical theatre auditions it's not uncommon to be asked to sing sixteen bars and then be let go: auditions can last thirty seconds. In the world of plays, auditions tend to run longer and actors are normally afforded a little more one-to-one conversation with the panel. I have seen some shocking behaviour from panellists in musical-theatre auditions, so I make a point to make it as stress-free and humane an experience for prospective actors or musicians as possible. Besides, as a composer you're desperate to find the right person for the job – you want the people coming in to be good. Treat them well or they may not take the job even if you offer it to them, and it will make it that much easier when you eventually start working together.

With actor-musicians, again, two contrasting pieces on their instrument and a song are the norm. Try to keep an open mind when they come in. You are basically trying to see if they are capable musicians and if they fit in your ensemble (casting directors and directors will also be looking at them from the perspective of acting ability and appearance). Try not to judge auditionees on their choice of audition material – they may do something completely contradictory to what you had in mind, but you never know what might inspire your score. Often I hear panels talking about bad choices of audition material, but the reality is that it can only be a bad choice if it doesn't show the auditionee off to the best of their ability. We won't be using this material in the show – I can use my imagination to work out if they can play as part of my ensemble. Don't discount people because they misinterpret your brief.

Unfortunately, a lot of auditionees are sent to auditions they are not really suited for. For example, actors' agents can sometimes take someone's limited experience of playing the recorder in high school to mean they are a proficient wind player. Actors should know better than to try and fake their way through a music audition, but sometimes they are pressurised by their agents to attend anyway. This ends up being a waste of everyone's time. The other thing that casting directors, composers and musical directors are wary of is when someone's CV appears to suggest they can play twenty instruments to professional standard. There may well be people out there who are so skilled, but in my experience this tends to be a gross overstatement. I have even heard on the grapevine that certain actor-musician courses encourage their students to pick up as many instruments as possible and if they can make a legitimate sound with them to put them on their CV. I would suggest that just because someone once touched a flute or saw a lyre does not mean that they can play it. In an ideal world, actor-musicians would only put the instruments on which they are technically proficient on their CV.

You might also come across the scenario where someone is cast who volunteers to 'learn' the instrument required during the rehearsal process. Depending on the level of complexity required of the piece this is often a bad idea. If the part calls for someone who has 'only just learned' to play the instrument then they will probably get away with it, but don't expect someone to become a professional-standard guitarist in a couple of months. Having said that, good actor-musicians are quite versatile where required on instruments of a similar nature to their principal instrument. For instance, I would have no problem casting a violinist who needs to play the viola (and hasn't before) or even a guitarist who has to learn the mandolin. (Even if a guitarist struggles with the different string-tuning between a mandolin and a guitar, they can retune it like the latter. It's a total cheat but can work wonders if necessary.) Weirdly, even something that seems so straightforward as a simple drum pattern can be tricky for a non-drummer to get a handle on. I would be wary of casting anyone who cites that because they passed their Grade 5 at school they are therefore experienced at playing an instrument. Ideally, you want to cast people who make a living as actor-musicians – who have played their instrument in a professional show before, and are able to hold their own as part of an ensemble.

Case Study: *The Recruiting Officer* at the Donmar Warehouse

One of the most fruitful experiences I have had so far when working with actor-musicians was with the Donmar Warehouse production of *The Recruiting Officer*. We auditioned a great many people for the five-part band in the show. What made these five men so special was that not only were they very good musicians with excellent singing capabilities, but that they could also, without exception, properly act. If you can seamlessly blend the musical prowess of five excellent performers into the fabric of a production where they are all crucial cast members who have important plot-driven roles, the results can be electric.

As I've mentioned previously, a lot of the music for *The Recruiting Officer* had to be written before the rehearsal period started. On day one of rehearsals, all five men and I went to a separate rehearsal studio along the road from the main building and set up camp to learn page upon page of the newly written folk-style music we would use for our twenty-minute pre-show sequence. This was quite a tough task for all, as it's no mean feat to memorise twenty minutes' worth of material that occurs before the play has even started. As with every big or difficult task, we broke it down into smaller sections and worked through it incrementally. Later in the same week, and at the same time as learning all of this music, the performers had to attend rehearsals with the rest of the company, learn their parts and then, of course, all the rest of the music that featured in the show. This was not a job for the faint-hearted. Had any of our instrumentalists not been confident in their ability to play their instruments they would have had a meltdown when we started to ask them to memorise the music, move whilst playing, remember lines, sing, act, change costume, remember cues, remember blocking, remember to leave an instrument in a certain area for a later cue, and remain on stage for the entire length of the show. When it works, a score played by actor-musicians can be completely magical, but it's by no means a picnic to achieve.

Once we had broken the back of the pre-show music and started working on the cues that would support the scene changes and glue the show together, the band spent more and more of their time in the rehearsal room. At the end of week one we did an informal performance of the music we had tackled so far for the rest of the acting company. This was a success and such a boost for the determination of all members of the production team that the energy the band created lasted not only for the rest of the rehearsal period but for the entire run itself.

Footage of this moment can be seen at youtu.be/MxY-gWl9XuE

Because we had built a band from separate parts (five actors who had until recently been complete strangers), and we wanted them to feel like a group that had been together for years, we decided that it would be a worthwhile exercise to perform a public gig before we got into the theatre. Everyone involved was equally committed to the concept of this production and could see the benefit of giving up an evening to play a free gig in the pub across the road from the rehearsal room. Getting the music out there (before it was properly ready perhaps) into a public forum and observing a visceral reaction from a crowd of strangers was, in this instance, the best boost to morale we could have hoped for. This very much encouraged the band to begin to feel like a unit that belonged together. Everyone returned to the rehearsal room the next day with a spring in their step and a renewed confidence that the production would work.

Whatever show you're working on, if you can find an appropriate way to maintain a level of anticipation or excitement around your score, then the actors or musicians in the show will respond several-fold. Music is a vital component in the creative process of theatre – in the case of *The Recruiting Officer* the rest of the company, which was full of well-known and experienced actors, could have reacted against this level of musical involvement or turned their noses up at the actor-musician element but, in fact, the opposite happened: the actor-musician band was the glue that bound this company together and the resulting production was all the better for it.

With *The Recruiting Officer*, I assumed the role of musical director for the rehearsal and technical period, and during previews. Obviously the band had to function on its own when on stage, do their own count-ins and collectively intuit their own cut-offs, but I was able to give notes after a performance from an outside perspective. Once the show had officially opened, I nominated one of them to take on the responsibility of musical director, but by this point they were so in tune with each other that this was only a formality. I would then see the show once every couple of weeks just to check it was still sounding up to scratch. With a show like this, the associate director will watch it often and report back, and you can always get a handle on any technical issues through the show reports, written after each performance by the stage-management team.

After a while, my attendance wasn't even necessary in order to note the band – they pretty much took care of themselves. I was only going to see the show to absorb their energy and enjoy their performances. It's a rare event when you feel so attached to a company you want to return to see the show again and again. For me, I think a large part of what made this production so special was the live-music element and the joy of seeing five top-notch actor-musicians working at the top of their game.

Act Four:

Performance

'To achieve great things, two things are needed: a plan, and not quite enough time.'

Leonard Bernstein

Collaborating

What is a Sound Designer?

Throughout this book there has been a lot of discussion about working with sound designers as it's likely that you will collaborate with them more than any other member of the creative team. In this chapter we'll look at their role in a little more detail.

Sound designers deal with both the technical and creative sound aspects of a production. Everything that an audience hears that comes from a source outside of the acting company will have crossed the sound designer's desk. Even live sounds will often be enhanced or amplified by the sound designer.

The sound designer is a key collaborator in the creative team. It's their job to create a sound world that supports and sits within the same realm as the other design aspects of the show. The Association of Sound Designers defines the role thus:

- The Sound Designer may create sound effects, atmospheres, sonic textures and filmic ambiences that will create naturalistic and abstract worlds for the show's story, as well as aid the audience's emotional and dramatic connection with the performance. This might also include the use of props onstage or other offstage effects.
- The Sound Designer may choose, edit and remix music; work with a composer to make original music; or work with live musicians in the theatre.
- The Sound Designer may advise on how to best hear the performers, which may involve acoustic adjustments to the

theatre and set, or the addition and configuration of radio and/or float mics for the performers.

- The Sound Designer will design a sound system, bespoke to the specific production and auditorium that will give the audience the best experience of the show.[62]

A sound designer will programme all music cues into the digital sound-cueing system or multimedia-playback software (commonly QLab), adjust levels and handle the mixing together of live and recorded music and sound. They will work with a team of engineers and technicians to balance a sound system in a theatre space. They can often be found negotiating with set designers or production managers about where on the set they can hide speakers, hang microphones or insert reverse-radio-systems – usually done with IEMs (in-ear monitors) connected to amps and speakers inside a prop as a way of producing sound from within them – without encumbering the playing space or being distracting or unsightly.

Defining Your Roles

The sound designer will become a close ally. Like composers, they may choose to spend some time with the acting company in the early days of rehearsal to participate in the research elements of the process. Depending on the remit of the show you may have less contact with the sound designer early on, but you'll always see them at production meetings once a week. As the rehearsal period progresses they're likely to be around more frequently, particularly in the last week. It's often the case that sound designers must juggle a larger number of overlapping projects than composers to keep themselves financially afloat. Composers often juggle several jobs at once too, but not typically as many as sound designers.

As you become more experienced, it's likely that you will come across the same creative team members time after time. Some sound designers will become regular collaborators and often directors will look to employ a sound designer and composer they know work well as a team. If you work well with a sound designer it's likely that you will form a bond of trust in each other's work and opinions, you will bounce ideas back and forth and sometimes look to each other for inspiration. Sharing a collective and challenging aim for a show can encourage you both to push yourselves out of your comfort zone and create something bold and new. These are the most rewarding relationships that produce the most interesting work. A good sound designer who connects with your ideas (and vice versa) will not let you settle for something below par: if you can trust each other and take each other's opinions objectively then you will both avoid the stagnation and complacency which can come with experience over time.

Composer-Sound Designers

There has been a trend in recent years for the combination composer-sound designer. These are flexible individuals who manage to span the remits of both jobs. Thrifty producers love this because they presumably imagine that they can only pay one set of fees, but I think that if someone is doing two jobs they should be compensated accordingly. In order to do both jobs effectively, an individual has to be incredibly highly skilled in two rather different areas. There are some who can do this, but in my experience most are noticeably more interested in one than the other. Many sound designers have no capacity to write music, and nor do they wish to. Likewise, speaking as a composer, I don't have the skill, technical prowess or patience to learn all that would be needed to become an effective sound designer. The trouble starts when those who work exclusively as a sound designer or composer are put out of work because producers would rather save money and employ an all-rounder. There are those who can do this but personally I still believe that theatre, being a collaborative art form, can benefit from the added expertise that comes from two pools of experience. Some shows are also so sound and music heavy that it would be almost impossible for one person to achieve everything to a world-class standard. I have always been very clear about the fact that I am not, nor will ever be, a sound designer.

Case Study: A Cautionary Tale

Once in my career, a theatre (without my knowledge) sent out a press release stating that I would be doing music *and* sound on a show of theirs. Almost instantly I received calls and emails from my peers asking if this was true. It was then, and still is, a contentious issue for those in the sound design and composition fields. I quickly called my agent who assured me that it was a mistake and that the theatre had promised that a sound designer would be hired. When I turned up on day one of rehearsal, I was surprised to hear that there was still no sound designer and the immortal words: 'Surely you will be able to work it out.'

This is maddening from the viewpoint of both fields and shows a lack of understanding about the separate roles. You don't become a sound designer overnight or by 'trying extra hard'. It takes years of experience and know-how to learn the skills required. Eventually, the theatre promised that their in-house head of sound would 'help me out'. Cue the alarm bells. Unfortunately this person was neither interested in nor bothered about the sound design for this play, and likewise in spending any time understanding its requirements or listening to my concerns. As far as I'm aware, he was not paid any extra to do the sound design so I went into the theatre as the 'idiot who took the job he can't do and expects the technical staff to help him out' guy.

The five minutes he spent putting my cues into the computer (QLab) system and the ten seconds he took to tell me that the sound system was not to be changed and any problems were to do with my music (when I queried the EQ levels on the system) were about all the support I got.

It's safe to say that not only was this process a horrible one, but I believe my work (and the resulting play) suffered. This production then transferred to another theatre and I still have vivid memories of running around listening to speakers, trying to balance and EQ them with next to no knowledge of what I was listening out for and without any technical support. Make sure you are clear what your job entails before you start. In this case, I may just as well have been doing the costume design.

Process

It is worth noting at this point that not every show you are employed to work on will require a huge amount of either music or sound design. It's less common as a composer to be employed on a show with next to no music (as savvy producers will try to avoid paying for anything unnecessary), but most shows will require some element of sound design no matter how simple. Sometimes as a composer you will be employed to write only what I lovingly term 'curtain-up-and-down-music' (or 'curtain music' as others call it) but you should try to find a way to make that process feel as inventive as possible. There are times as a composer when you feel underused, but chances are there's another interesting 'seat-of-the-pants-style-impossibly-terrifying' project lurking just around the corner. Over the span of a career I think the complicated and straightforward jobs probably balance themselves out.

Normally, you will have had a dialogue with the sound designer near the beginning of rehearsals about the general sound world of the production. It may be that this develops clarity quickly over time or it may that you have no idea what you're going to do until you're well into the rehearsal process. In any case, it's important to keep that dialogue open so that when either of you come across helpful or instructive clues about what the production aims to be, you can keep each other in the loop.

The sound designer will normally keep you abreast of any relevant technical issues that might come up regarding the concept during production meetings, but they tend not to need to concern you with details of the general set-up. When setting up the sound system in the theatre they will have designated 'quiet time' to balance, EQ and set time-delays and a few initial levels for cues. This session is regularly never as quiet as it should be due to people trampling in and out of the space and occasionally trying to drill in a sneaky screw or two. Sometimes at the end of the session they will play your newly composed music through the theatre system for the first time.

Don't be alarmed if the first time you hear your music through the theatre speakers it doesn't sound how you expected, as the sound designer will still be balancing the sound in the space. They can adjust the system and levels of track to send to certain speakers – for example, the level of low frequency playing through the sub-bass can dramatically affect the mix across a large theatre system.

Most of the time, you will want to remix your tracks after you've heard them in the theatre. The mix you get on your home speakers or headphones is a good place to start as a general guide, but remember that this is music for the support of the theatrical experience – it needs to work in the theatre. As you begin to understand how it sounds in the space, you will use the time during the technical rehearsal to adapt your mixing parameters. Be aware though that once the tech has started there are lots of people vying for time to get technical (and sometimes dangerous) jobs done. It's not always appropriate to play loud sound cues in the auditorium. The sound department will be allocated quiet time which you can partly use for detailed music balancing.

Using Stems

When we looked at the recording process, we came across the use of stems. These are versions of the track that are usefully broken down into instrument groupings that can be placed into a system together to recreate the whole piece. It can be useful, if you have a large track that you know will require specific mixing in the theatre, to give the sound designer the track as stems and listen to the mix this way. You can then adjust the levels of different instrument groups as you listen to get the best balance in the theatre. It's good practice to go back to your original files and adjust the full mix accordingly.

Combining Music and Sound Effects

We previously touched on the idea that sometimes you'll want to write music that incorporates sound effects. Even when you do this, the sound designer may want to separately control the different sound elements in the theatre. It may be that you want to stem the music and sound effects separately or that the sound designer wants to further enhance those that are a part of the music. Often, a sound designer will add sound effects on top of the music after you have provided it, sometimes leading into the set-up of a scene or to counterbalance the music cue with something firmly planted in the reality of the scene change. You shouldn't be afraid to suggest ideas to each other at this point. Try not to become overly attached to, or precious about, your music. A good sound designer can add an extra level of ambience to a cue with some cleverly placed atmospheres, textures, soundscapes or sound effects.

MIDI-ing Cues

QLab can also act as an essential hub to synchronise with the other creative departments. If you want a lighting cue to occur at exactly the same time as a note or sound, then the two cues can be linked together using MIDI (Musical Instrument Digital Interface). This is the same MIDI that keyboards and software synthesisers communicate with. The MIDI control is handled by the sound designer who programs it such that when the sound is cued, the lights are also cued instantaneously. This makes it possible to do any number of precise sound and music synchronisations, which can be used to striking effect.

Vamping Cues

Another feature of the programming tool that a sound designer will utilise is the vamp. 'Vamping' is a term coined from music that relates to a particular section of bars that are repeated until otherwise instructed. You can program a pre-recorded music cue to repeat on loop under a scene. When you need to move on you then 'de-vamp' and link to a new section of music.

Case Study: *Privacy* at the Donmar Warehouse

One of the more complex vamping cues I've seen was in our Donmar Warehouse production of *Privacy*. The section in question was a series of monologues underscored by a twelve-bar jazz pattern. At specific points during the monologues, other musical riffs (drum fills or cymbal splashes) were added to emphasise a line or action whilst the jazz pattern kept running. In order for this to work they would have to happen in tempo and exactly in time with the vamping music. To do this, our sound designer set up individual (very short) vamps for each of these cymbal splashes or drum fills, which ran silently in time and tempo alongside the track that was playing. When they were cued they would synchronise perfectly with the underscore vamp and then play out. Without the benefit of a live band to follow the dialogue for cues, this was a good way to get the same desired result.

Mic'ing

The sound designer will also oversee the setting up of actors with the necessary microphones. They will help balance and EQ them in the theatre, but will pass the mixing responsibility onto the sound operator. It's normal practice to hide these mics on the lapels of actors' jackets or in their hairline. Every scenario calls for an individual approach, but I've seen (or not seen) some incredibly well-hidden mics on actors in close proximity to an audience. This makes me despair when I see huge, badly hidden microphones taped to actors' faces.

When we mic'd the actors for *The Recruiting Officer* at the Donmar, every microphone and cable was carefully hand-coloured to blend with the particular actor's hair-colour and skin-tone, making them nearly impossible for an audience to detect. It's necessary when you're setting a show in the eighteenth century not to interrupt an audience's suspension of disbelief by inelegantly sticking microphones everywhere. However, it does depend on the style and volume of music as to what kind of microphone can be used. These small and discreet microphones were perfect for our relatively quiet eighteenth-century folk music. If, however, you're doing a rock opera then you may not have this luxury. Sometimes, larger and more conspicuous equipment is needed, but, for what it's worth, I still feel that it's always worth trying to make the inclusion of microphones as aesthetically compatible with a production's design values as possible.

Sound Levels

It is constantly surprising to me how much the presence of an audience changes the balance of sound in a theatre space. Human bodies soak up sound, so it's common to feel like the music level in a technical or dress rehearsal (without an audience) is far too loud. This is hardly ever the case once the theatre is full. It usually takes a couple of preview performances to plot an exact level for all music cues. Not only do bodies soak up sound but you also have to take into consideration the general hubbub that audiences make as the show is starting and the applause during the curtain call. This is, however, one of the more straightforward parts of the process. During the West End production of *Much Ado About Nothing*, the audience were so excitable by the finale that the extreme sound level we had to plot was completely unbearable to listen to in the empty theatre.

Using Found Music

A sound designer can source music if a play requires a particular existing song or recording. A theatre producer or general manager will inform the Performing Rights Society of any music used that has not been specifically commissioned for their production. There are a few different circumstances you may come across.

The Performing Rights Society (www.prsformusic.com) grants licences to all public spaces that wish to play music. The Copyright, Designs and Patents Act 1988 states you need to get permission from the copyright holder to 'perform' music in public – and a music licence grants you this permission.[63]

The PRS grant licences to theatres for the following:

- Overture, Entr'acte and Exit Music requires a PRS blanket music licence, which every public venue requires to play music of any kind. For theatres, this is paid at a fixed rate (considered an annual royalty) dependent on the size and location of the venue, being defined as permanent repertory theatres, provincial and London suburban theatres or London West End theatres.
- Incidental or Curtain Music. This is music used to add atmosphere to action or to be used for scene changes within a stage play. This requires a PRS licence and a (fixed) weekly royalty payment to the PRS dependent on the size and location of the theatre.
- Concerts at which copyright material is performed also require a PRS licence except for complete concert

performances of dramatico-musical works. (These are licensed by the individual copyright owner.)[64]

- Musical excerpts from dramatico-musical works (including operas, operettas, musical plays, revues and pantomimes whose music is specially written for them) are sometimes woven into performances. The PRS only controls this music when it is performed 'non-dramatically'. It does not have control when it is dramatically performed. A performance is viewed as being dramatic where there is any portrayal of the writer's original conception of the work from which the excerpt is taken – i.e. through any accompanying dramatic action whether acted, danced or mimed or through the use of costume, scenery or other visual effects.[65]

Interpolated Music

The PRS defines this as 'music not specially written for a particular theatrical production but performed by a character(s) to be heard by another character(s) in that production'. For this you need to gain clearance through the PRS, although it could mean you negotiate directly with the copyright owner. You must notify the PRS of your intention to use a piece of interpolated music at least thirty days before your production is due to start. This gives them time to contact the copyright owner of the music who has to approve its use. You must specify:

- The manner of the performance.
- The duration of the performance.
- The name of the production.
- The dates of performances.
- The venues in which the performances will take place.

If permission is not granted before the start date of the performance then the music cannot be used as part of the production. The royalties payable for use of interpolated music depend on the duration of that music in relation to the total running time (excluding interval) of the theatrical production and on the size and location of the theatre.

The Performing Rights Society does not control what are known as Grand Rights. These are performances of ballets or dramatico-musical works whose music is written especially for them, e.g. musical plays, operas, operettas, revue and pantomimes. The PRS does not control the performance of a complete musical or other music written specially for a theatrical production as in incidental music written specially for a play. The PRS does, however, handle rights if these are performed by means of a film or broadcast on radio or television.[66]

Most of the time it's the responsibility of the producer to deal with the PRS, but it's worth keeping abreast of how the process is going. You may need to replace music very quickly if you've been denied a licence to use it.

As a side note, if you have any music recorded and released and you don't have a music publisher then you should make sure you register every piece individually with the PRS. This will ensure you are paid the appropriate royalties should someone else wish to use it in any medium – theatre, film, radio or television.

Getting the Show On

Theatre Fit-Up

Depending on the theatre, the fit-up schedule will vary. For plays, the process of replacing an old production with a new one tends to happen very quickly. At the Donmar Warehouse, the typical fit-up schedule is lightning quick and runs something like this:

On the Saturday night, the final show of the previous production finishes. Immediately after the audience vacates the auditorium the 'get-out' starts. The old set is dismantled and removed and any necessary painting of the back wall is done. The new set is then put into the theatre on the Sunday – the 'get-in'. As this is happening, flies equipment and lighting equipment are rigged. On the Monday as the set and lighting rigs are being finalised, the sound system is rigged. By mid-afternoon the lighting designer and his team will begin the process of focusing lights. Then in the evening the sound designer is allocated quiet time to calibrate the sound system and try out a few music cues in the space. Tuesday morning is the continuation of technical work on stage, and the technical rehearsal with all actors and creative staff begins on Tuesday afternoon. There is normally an orientation talk from the theatre manager to the acting company, followed by a 'walk-round' of the set and building to familiarise the actors with the playing area and the auditorium. After this is all taken care of, the technical rehearsal can begin.

Production Desks and Essential Equipment

For the technical rehearsal, you will normally be allocated a production desk in the auditorium. Sometimes you will be required to share this with the sound designer, but as they tend to have quite a lot of equipment, it's best to have your own allotted space. This should be in close proximity to the sound designer so you can interact with each other continually throughout the tech. As you become more experienced you will work out what your ideal production desk set-up is. I normally take an external mouse and keyboard to make editing on a laptop slightly easier. I also take a small MIDI controller keyboard and sustain pedal in case I have to do a quick MIDI recording and add to or edit cues. Try to make your technical-rehearsal process as stress-free as possible – you don't want to get stranded without the ability to record small additions to your music cues quickly. Increasingly these days, sound designers are able to network your computers together so you can share files instantly, but it's best to keep a small USB stick around just in case there are any hiccups with the networking system. You will also need a good pair of headphones for mixing during the tech. Always have your script and some notepaper handy.

Dry Tech

'Dry tech' is the term used for a process where the technical and creative team try out complex scene changes or technical automation without any actors present. With plays, this tends to happen on the morning of the first day of the technical rehearsal. The dry tech will be run by the stage manager and involve members of the stage-management team. They won't normally require lights or sound for this process (especially when they're just working out logistics), but it gives a good indication of how the scene change is actually going to work and how long it might take. It's always useful to gain a head start before you reach this part of the play in the tech. If there is time, the stage-management team might run this sequence several times over and give you the opportunity to try it with lights and sound. If it's a scene change involving lots of set and prop movements, it will be at its slowest at this rehearsal. As the crew become more accustomed to the technical aspects of the change, they will work out ways to make it faster. Speed is of the essence here – as we know, if a scene change doesn't incorporate any narrative elements then it needs to happen as quickly as possible, no matter how entertaining your music is.

The Technical Rehearsal

Each day of the tech is split up into three sessions for actors and creatives. Various technical staff work in shifts and can often be called overnight to complete a paint call or any set maintenance. Typically tech sessions are three or three-and-a-half hours long with a fifteen-minute tea break. One of the quirks of tech means that actors are required to have fifteen minutes to get into costume at the beginning of a session and fifteen minutes to get out of it again at the end. This gives you extra time at either end of a session to update and test cues through the sound system. When working with live bands (if they aren't required to be in costume for tech) you can sometimes use this time for a sneaky music rehearsal. This can be invaluable if you are involved in a tightly scheduled tech.

When you begin the first tech session, it's likely that one of the first things in the show is a music and lighting cue. You should try to liaise with the lighting designer beforehand so that you have (at the very least) the first cue of the show ready to go. Communication between all the creative departments is crucial for a smoothly running tech but, most importantly, make sure you are in constant contact with the sound designer, the lighting designer and the deputy stage manager (DSM) who is on the book and calling all cues. You will be given cans to wear that allow you to talk to all departments easily, but in my experience if too many people are talking over the system at once it can get a little crowded. A lot of the time it is best to talk your notes through with the sound designer (and if it's a recorded score, he will have to put your cues into the system anyway) and allow him to liaise with the DSM about notes or cue points. If you can get several cues programmed before each technical session it will make the whole process run more smoothly and quickly. The last thing you want is for your department to eat up precious tech time because you haven't been ahead of the game. Of course, there may be many technical elements to synchronise in the opening cue, and this may take some time, but don't let it be because you were unprepared. Once you have your first cue in the bag and it doesn't require any immediate editing, make sure you are set up for the next one and stay several cues ahead. Bear in mind that sound designers have a lot more going on than just programming the music cues you give them, so stay patient and be aware of when is a good time to discuss the next musical moment.

Technical rehearsals can be invigorating if you have lots of cues in quick succession. Sometimes you may think you have all your cues ready, but you'll almost always have edits to make as the tech progresses and it's common practice for a director to ask for something completely new. You must be prepared to write on the fly and create new cues by editing and augmenting the elements you already have. If you're working with a recorded score this is where your many alternative cues will come in handy. You may have recorded bits of music that you never thought you'd require, but suddenly there will come a use for every scrap of audio you have. Don't ever delete anything – you never know when it might come in useful.

The Rest of the Creative Team

During the tech, the director will be busy working with both the cast and the creative team simultaneously. It's not uncommon for them to give a note to one creative department that will directly affect another, but they won't always have time to explain it to each individually or call a group meeting. Departments will have to communicate and come up with a collective solution that works for all. Quite often, if you change a music cue it will necessitate a change in lighting (either the lighting cue itself or the cue point). Likewise, if a piece of video changes, it is likely that the music will have to change to sync up with it.

Never take for granted that the other departments will do what you expect. You may think you have come up with the best solution for a moment, but others may have different ideas or other factors to consider that you are unaware of. For this reason, you should foster a relationship with the lighting designer (for example) that encourages you both to share ideas as you track through the tech. If you plan to 'button' a music cue going into a scene, it's likely that the lighting designer will want to know about that, as will the DSM. It's normally quicker for a lighting designer to change his cue to fit the music, but that doesn't mean that it's the music that is correct or should be followed. Keep an open mind in technical rehearsals. Even though you may think that you've recorded all the music by this point, the job is far from over. Whole scores have been changed during technical rehearsals and previews, and although this can be highly stressful it's a necessary process to make the show the best it can possibly be.

Working with Video Designers

Implementing changes in video design tends to take slightly longer than with other creative departments as the process of exporting the files (known as rendering) requires incredibly large amounts of data to be processed. Bear this in mind before getting impatient with video designers.

Case Study: *Privacy* at the Donmar Warehouse

Josie Rourke's production of James Graham's play *Privacy* utilised an incredible amount of video projection. Almost all the video required a soundtrack, whether it was music or sound design. As this play was so 'up-to-the-minute' with regards its subject matter, the script continually evolved throughout the rehearsal process. The show featured lots of audio-visual set pieces, and there was a team of video designers working on the project pretty much around the clock. The musical score of the play had to develop as the production did, but it also had to sync with both the stylistic language of the video and exact cue points. As always happens, a sizeable portion of the video and sound content was created towards the end of the rehearsal period. The volume of work required and the length of time it took to create it pushed what would be the normal creative schedule to the wire.

The period just before you start teching a very complex show can be a hectic time. Every creative department is trying to plough through all their necessary cues to arrive at tech with at least a draft of something to contribute. Communication between departments is key here, particularly if there are lots of video and music cues to sync up. Everyone is working on different parts of the same cues; the problem is, when time is so limited and people are working in different locations, some details can slip through the cracks. Just trying to get clarification on how everyone is tackling a particular moment can be tricky, and holding meetings about it doesn't necessarily throw up complete answers. This is because in the process of creating a cue you constantly have to make decisions: if, for example, the decision you make will affect how the music will sync with video or vice versa, you need to be able to get a response quickly from the other departments or be in the same room creating together. Even just sending large files to each other can eat up precious time. What inevitably happens is that you all create 'something' in the hope that when you put it together you can work out how to combine the various elements. Of course, this is not an ideal working situation, but sometimes you just have to go with it. If you are trying to score music to picture, it helps a great deal to have the picture to sync up with.

In an ideal world everyone would create their work in the same place, but because each department has its own unique technical requirements that's very difficult. Things do become easier when all departments are physically forced to be in the theatre together for the technical rehearsal.

Dress Rehearsals

Normally you will have time for one dress rehearsal and it will be on the afternoon of the first preview performance. Depending on the scope of the technical aspects of your show, you may be in the fortunate position where you are afforded more than one. This is a rare event, however – most of the time you are very much against the clock to finish the tech in time. If a play consists of only a few scenes in similar locations and doesn't feature a great amount of technical business with actors, set changes or props then it's more likely you will have some time to spare. I was once in the situation that the technical rehearsal went so smoothly and swiftly that there would have been time for three dress rehearsals (and this was on a normal tech schedule).

The director wisely decided to have only two dress rehearsals: at a certain point, a show needs an audience.

Dress rehearsals are treated very much like show performances and will not stop unless specifically requested to do so by the stage manager or director, normally for safety or important technical reasons. Use dress rehearsals to make any major notes on music, but be aware that it's unlikely you will have time to change much before your production desk needs to be cleared from the auditorium in preparation for a public audience. If there is a major disaster then you should take the chance to rectify it before opening to the public, but be aware that the sound and lighting designers will also be implementing their own critical changes so time is of the essence. Keep your notes safe and refer to them again after the first preview and see if the presence of an audience changes your opinion at all.

Previews

During previews, it is likely that you will be given the opportunity to sit in different seats in the auditorium for different performances. For the composer and sound designer this is an opportunity to check that the sound and music work in all areas of the theatre. Of course every position in the house will have a slightly different experience, but the quality of the sound must remain constant. I normally prefer to sit next to the sound designer for previews so we can get a shared experience and discuss afterwards. Listen out for the balance of your music in different areas – it may be that what sounded a bit too bass-heavy in the stalls will sound empty in the circle. A sound designer will address these discrepancies accordingly.

Use previews to gauge the audience reaction to the show as a whole, but with specific reference to your music cues. Does a scene change maintain the energy of the play or does it sag? Does the music deliver the scene in the best way to engage the audience? How does the presence of an audience affect the mood of a scene? Does the music support the storytelling? Are music and sound-design elements sympathetic to one another? Does the music feel a part of the show rather than something external? Is the music ever in the way of a moment? Does another moment require music?

Take a notebook with you to keep track of all your music cues and anything else you notice that may be particular to where you are sitting. It is not your job to note other departments, but if you spot something you think is critical and that others might not have clocked from elsewhere in the house it might be worth quietly mentioning it, but only if you're sure it's appropriate to do so. It can also be worthwhile to eavesdrop on audience members' conversations as they leave the theatre: learn things about their experience that you would otherwise never be privy to. If they don't know who you are you can even ask questions if you want to. A word of warning though – there's no guarantee that the things they will be saying will be complimentary. Try to remain objective at all times and use this feedback to improve the show.

Technical Notes

'Tech notes' happen after every preview performance, usually in the auditorium immediately after the audience has cleared. They are run by the production manager and attended by all creative departments. This is an opportunity for immediate feedback on the technical aspects of that evening's show. Normally it is the director who will give their notes first and then each creative department will bring up anything else that has not been covered. Holding this meeting directly after the show ensures memories are fresh and any technical issues that need to be addressed for the next performance can be scheduled for the following day.

Rehearsals During Previews

It is common that the morning sessions during previews are used for technical work without actors. There are set rules on how long actors' and technical staff's breaks are required to be between the end of the evening performance and the following day's rehearsal, but it is common for creatives to be back in the theatre at 10 a.m. if not earlier. Actors normally arrive for an afternoon session on stage (after notes with the director) where any technical issues can be resolved and their on-stage notes can be addressed.

At the end of each evening you'll have a list of notes you'll want to implement the next day. Be careful not to adjust anything that will directly affect either actors or other technical departments without first clearing it with the director, the DSM and the people involved. If, for example, you make a music cue shorter, you need to make sure that everyone affected is aware, and then technically rehearse it, or you may end up with a disaster on your hands in front of a public audience. The music may no longer work with the lighting, or you run the risk of throwing an actor completely off-balance, which isn't fair. If you have specific notes that you know will need to be rehearsed on stage, try to let the director or assistant director know either at tech notes or as early in the morning of the next day as possible. They can then plot this into their rehearsal schedule. If they can't fit into the rehearsal then you should not put in the change for that evening's performance. One of the toughest things about the preview period is when you know that something isn't right, but you're unable to change it before the next performance. You then have to watch the show again with an audience, knowing that a part of your work is flawed but remains unfixed.

Sometimes, even after you think all your music cues are working and the show is holding together, you'll find other elements start to change that can affect the score. If, for example, after several performances the pace of the show quickens, you may want to shorten cues or even replace them if they are no longer supporting the drive of the drama. It may be that a button that once provoked a laugh no longer does so and in fact tramples the natural laugh an actor is receiving at the end of a scene. This is why it is important to remain engaged with the process and never become complacent. If you are afforded a long preview period, you may ask permission from the director to take an evening off which will hopefully give you a new sense of perspective the next day when you see the show. Sometimes productions are 'frozen' after a number of previews, which means the creative team's work is finished even though the show has not officially reached its opening night. This gives the company a chance to 'own' the production, settle into their performances and let the production 'breathe' without constant changes every day. Freezing the show is sometimes necessary to prevent it from becoming 'over-tampered' with.

Opening Night

Opening night, also known as press night (when the press traditionally attend the performance and write their reviews) is your last official night working on the show. Traditionally these performances start earlier than usual in order for the press to leave the theatre as early as possible and get their reviews ready to publish the next day. Normally in the UK, unless your production is incredibly long, a press-night performance starts at 7 p.m. As a composer you are usually given two tickets for press night (so you can take a guest), but it is up to you if you want to watch the actual performance. Directors, designers, sound designers, lighting designers, composers; they are all powerless on press night, so they can either soak up the atmosphere and enjoy the show or they can prop up the bar across the street. I like to attend the show on press night so I can see the particular performance the critics will write about. It also means I have a shared experience with other audience members to talk about after the show.

Hopefully, as it's press night (and at the end of the day it is 'show business') there will be a party afterwards. This is an opportunity to celebrate all the work of every department, including technical, theatre and production staff. It may be the last opportunity you have to socialise with the creative team and acting company before you head off on your next adventure, so celebrate together and enjoy the party. Press-night parties often have a weird energy of anticipation about them: everyone is aware that the reviews will be published imminently. In the past, reviews would be published in the early hours of the next morning, so these parties could be interrupted by the arrival of a glowing or ghastly review. These days, due to social media, they can arrive even earlier than that. Be careful not to share reviews with members of the company unless you know they read them. A lot of actors choose not to read reviews, which is completely understandable when you consider they have to perform in the show eight times a week for subsequent months. Even praise can have a detrimental effect on a performance, changing an actor's perspective and interrupting their natural or rehearsed choices. As a member of the creative team it is up to you whether or not you read reviews. I tend to read them as I want to be able to reflect on the show's perks and pitfalls and to see if I agree with a critic's summation. Treat it as a learning opportunity, but try not to take any of it too seriously. It can be very upsetting to get a bad review, but if you're proud of the work then you shouldn't dwell on what is essentially just one more opinion.

There is an increasing trend (if a show is ready in time) to invite theatre critics to attend performances before, rather than directly on, the opening night. Spreading the critics' attendance like this presents a more balanced opportunity for the show to be critiqued fairly, slightly alleviating the pressure of one single performance. If something technical goes horribly wrong by sheer chance on press night, it would be unfortunate if this hampered a good show's potential for success, but I would like to think that most critics understand the live nature of theatre and will not let it sway them too much when considering their verdict.

There is a tradition before the press performance of giving first-night cards to those you've worked with – cast, crew, creative team and perhaps theatre staff you've worked with. Whether you do this is up to you but it's likely that others will, so it's always best to come prepared.

After Opening

Usually after press night a composer's work is done, but some shows you may need to check on (mostly those with live music). I enjoy checking in on shows if they happen to be on in the vicinity, especially if I have had a particularly pleasant experience with a company. You will be kept up to speed on every performance by the show report. This is a document emailed by the company manager or DSM after every performance detailing such things as technical issues, audience reactions, understudy performances, performance times and audience numbers. It is normally a nice email to receive as it keeps you in the loop and reminds you that somewhere in the world there was an audience enjoying a production you worked on.

Highs and Lows

I think it's important to say a few words about the part of the creative process that some people find a little difficult to talk about. Sometimes, when working on a score (and this happens to me at some point on every show) you may feel that you've lost all ability to compose and can't produce anything you think worthwhile. In my own experience this is usually because I haven't given myself a clear enough brief.

If you're sitting at your piano and nothing seems to be happening, good advice is to take a break and not force it. Great advice is to re-examine what it is you think you're meant to be writing. Sometimes the reason that nothing is happening is because you are not allowing yourself to make decisions. As I've mentioned already, I believe there is a fundamental stage of composing that is all about the basics of which note and which harmony. If nothing is happening, then maybe you haven't a clear enough notion of what it is you're meant to be writing in the first place. Go back to your brief. And never underestimate the stymying power of fear. The best thing is just to get on and create 'something'. As Walt Disney famously said: 'The best way to get started is to stop talking and begin doing.'[67]

When working on a score, there are sometimes moments where everything flows so wonderfully that you lose complete track of time and are carried away in the process of creating music. Sometimes it feels like a total slog. Don't allow yourself to be put off by these harder periods. Everyone finds it difficult a lot of the time. No one's alone in finding the creative process challenging. If it is 80% procrastination, 18% perspiration and only 2% inspiration, so what? If in the time you have, you've created a brand new piece of art, however small, then you're already on a different planet to the rest of us who have produced nothing that day.

And yes, the highs are incredible. If you have a hit show and a glitzy press-night party to look forward to, then 'them's the perks', as they say. But it's normal to have a bit of a downer when all the hype has died down. You leave the production family, they carry on with their show and you move on to something else – sometimes nothing much in particular. This is all in the nature of working in the arts. But if you're aware it happens, try not to let it get on top of you. Keep busy, carry on and you'll be all right.

Transfers

Sometimes, successful shows move theatres (or tour) and the original creative team is engaged to remount them. Normally at this point a composer's involvement is minimal, as once the music is set (especially with a recorded score) it is set. Occasionally I have had to re-edit scene-change music when a show has transferred theatres because the technical specifications of the building were different, meaning a scene change took a longer or shorter time to complete. If the music in the scene change ends with a fade-out, it may mean that no changes are required, but if it tells a particular story and needs to have a definite ending, it's better to re-edit it. This is not normally a huge job; not like writing the music in the first place and rather pleasingly (or not) it gives you a chance to re-examine your work. This is not an opportunity to make any major changes to your score, but little bits of tightening here and there will make the minimal extra effort worthwhile.

Cinema Broadcasts

Cinema broadcasts of live theatre events are becoming more and more popular. Companies leading the way most notably are NT Live and RSC Live from Stratford-upon-Avon. They capture live theatre performances in high quality using multiple cameras, and instantly stream them worldwide. These broadcasts give a much wider audience a chance to see a stage show they would otherwise have missed. Some critics think that theatre performances belong in the theatre and that by putting a theatre show on screen you are detracting from the real thing. They cite ideas such as the unspoken pact between performer and audience being broken, the audience being told what to watch by the camera director, and that actors' performances in the theatre are, by necessity, larger than you would expect on screen and will therefore come across as 'untruthful'. Whilst some might argue these to be valid points, I think that cinema audiences are aware that they are watching a theatre performance and not a movie, and will still be carried away on a journey if the storytelling is strong enough. It also makes the theatre-going experience much more democratic, enabling far more people to experience a piece of art for a lower price and always from the best seat in the house. Some other critics believe that by screening high-quality, affordable, world-class theatre to cinemas around the country, the regional theatres will suffer. It would seem that this is not the case. Research carried out by the innovation foundation Nesta found that NT Live has 'on average grown audiences for local theatre in London and has had a neutral impact regionally'.[68]

There are also companies that record several performances of a particular show over a few days and cut them together to make one show. As the composer of a theatre piece that is filmed it is unlikely that you will have to get involved with the filming process or make any changes. You are normally welcome to attend the camera rehearsal and give notes (along with the sound designer), but there is no requirement to. From a financial perspective, it is likely that you will receive an upfront payment for this broadcast and be allocated points in the royalty pool, should it make a profit.

Case Study: *The Vote* at the Donmar Warehouse – and on More4

In 2015 I was fortunate to compose music for a fascinating experiment in broadcasting and theatre where a real-time play was broadcast live from the Donmar on the free-to-view digital television channel More4. *The Vote* by James Graham was set during the last ninety minutes of polling on election night and was accurately timed so that the performance would come down exactly at 10 p.m. with the chimes of Big Ben as the polls closed. From a technical standpoint the show had its challenges: the play continued in the theatre during the compulsory advert breaks where the television audience would cut away, so the 'theatre-only content' had to be timed to the second. It was also a show with a cast of over forty actors, which in the tiny Donmar space was an experiment in itself. Being broadcast on More4 meant that it was readily available to the nation from the comfort of their sofas and with over half a million viewers it broke viewing figures for both the Donmar (where the previous record was 180,000 for the NT Live broadcast of *Coriolanus*)[69] and for the channel itself (grossing the largest More4 audience of the year for the slot).[70]

Whether or not this will lead to many more live-theatre-on-television screenings we'll have to wait and see, but it's clear that with the success of cinema broadcasts and *The Vote*, the landscape of British theatre on screen is changing. Allowing thousands of additional people to see productions that they would otherwise have missed out on is a good thing. As long as the research continues into how, as it progresses, it affects small-scale touring and regional theatre, then we should embrace it in the same way as the public (as evidenced by the viewing figures) clearly have done.

Act Five:

Work
(*and How to Get It*)

‘A creative artist works on his next composition because he was not satisfied with his previous one.’

Dmitri Shostakovich

The Route

When people ask me how I started to write music for plays, they are often surprised by the sheer extent of happenstance and luck that led me down this particular road. I don't think I'm unusual in that I didn't set out to write music for plays. After teaching myself the piano as a child, I longed for a career in songwriting: pop music primarily and then later musical theatre. I went to a performing arts college (Liverpool Institute for Performing Arts) to study music and for the first couple of years only occasionally participated in any theatre activities. Even when I did decide to concentrate my efforts on musical theatre it never occurred to me that there might be a world of plays out there that required composers. In fact, it took me a long time to even call myself a composer – I was a songwriter; the word 'composer' seemed far too hifalutin. In my secondary-school music class, composition was called 'inventing' (presumably because we couldn't possibly declare the music we were sweating out as 'composition'). No, that required formal music education in a building with a royal crest on the front of it – surely?

The truth is, concert works, musicals, films, albums all seem to be much more glamorous and financially rewarding (although they often aren't) than writing music for plays. Composition in the 'straight theatre' can act as a training ground for any of those projects, but it is frequently wholly satisfying in itself. Plays, more than any other compositional work, demand a strong multi-purpose technique, openness for collaboration, an eclectic knowledge and a keen interest in storytelling. If you're going to write music for plays, you need to be able to turn your hand to almost anything musically and because of that, the people who do compose music for the theatre get there by a myriad of different pathways and circumstances. Many Oscar-winning composers still write music for theatre in between film projects. As you might expect, there is no tried-and-tested route to becoming a theatre composer.

As a young composer in London, having previously served as an assistant musical director, I was busy writing small-scale musical theatre and cabaret when I received a last-minute call to participate in a podcast discussion about new musical theatre. A contemporary of mine who was meant to be on the panel became unavailable at the last minute and for some reason (I can't remember why now) they called me. On the panel was a representative from the Arts Council who was very intrigued by the mention of an idea for a 'composer-in-residence' scheme. He later asked me to carry on the discussion over coffee. From what seemed like out of nowhere he managed to procure me an invitation to visit the Bush Theatre with a view to becoming their first composer-in-residence.

The Bush Theatre is a world-leading new-writing powerhouse and it became my home for the next two years. Yes, I wrote a musical there, but even more fascinating was my introduction to a world of drama I had neglected to embrace. There has been a tendency amongst some musical-theatre writers (and I was one of them) to become engrossed in an insular musical-theatre world, when right next door there is an entire industry of playwrights and directors putting on world-class productions of plays. I think it's exceedingly important that artists get as broad a spectrum of inspiration and education as possible, and one of the best places to get that is at the theatre. After forming many friendships and professional relationships at the Bush I was offered a job as composer-in-residence at the Donmar Warehouse. It was my relationship with Josie Rourke, the artistic director of both of those institutions, that led me to writing music for plays in the first place. In doing that, I have been fortunate enough to work steadily with some of the leading directors and playwrights, in the leading theatres, with the leading actors, ever since. The capacity for learning whilst working on these kinds of jobs with these kinds of people is unparalleled. You can never rest on your laurels when scoring plays, because you never know what the next moment will call for. You can't just churn out the same thing every time because you are being constantly challenged to respond to the specific needs of the production. This is the best training you could ask for.

Directors are the people who usually have the power to hire composers. A director will specify their preferred creative team to a producer or producing theatre who can, in turn, suggest their own ideas. Sometimes a producer might question the employment of someone who perhaps is untested in the theatrical forum, but mostly, if a director trusts in a composer to deliver, the producer will back him up. Meeting directors may seem like a tricky thing to set up, but your best bet is to start working on small projects either at school, in college or in your local community and invite people to see your work. If you've got the option to watch a lot of theatre, then do so. To some extent this is harder if you don't live in London or don't have lots of spare cash to burn, but there are great regional theatres around the country producing top-quality work. Also, don't forget that cinema broadcasts of theatre productions make them far more accessible on a budget from wherever you are in the world. Absorb all the influences you can: get to know which directors' work you enjoy and write to them. You could even send a director a demo or two. What's the worst that could happen?

The most important thing to do is to get some experience on your CV. It doesn't matter if it's in a town hall or on Broadway. If you can show some proclivity for hard work, directors are much more likely to take you seriously. Take every job going and turn your hand to as many styles of music as you can. Even after years of working I still have difficulty turning things down: I am constantly thrilled when someone decides they would like me to write the music for their show. Never take anything for granted. The number of weird and wonderful jobs I took on as a young composer and musical director is still staggering to me now. From the cramped and seedy nightclubs of Soho to commercials for car insurance, there's something to learn from every experience, so no matter how far from your desired path a music job might seem, you should take it on, make the most of it and feel proud to be earning a pay cheque. You will meet new people every time you take on a new project, and you never know where those relationships might lead. Always remember that the theatre industry is small: contacts are vital to keep your workload ticking over and you never know who might come to see your latest offering or what new opportunities lie right around the corner.

Making a Living

It probably comes as no surprise that composing music for plays is unlikely to turn you into a millionaire. Composers are self-employed and therefore have to take on lots of projects (which often overlap) to make a decent living. Fees vary depending on producers, production scales and budgets. At the time of writing, a professional production will normally pay you a fee somewhere between £1,500 and £6,000 to write the score for a play. As you become more experienced, that might go up, but most producing houses have set guidelines for what they pay across the board. It is common practice for your fee to be split into chunks and paid a third on signature of your contract, a third on the first day of rehearsals, and a third on press night.

Sometimes you will also be entitled to other payments or royalties. Each producer will negotiate these on an individual basis:

- A 'weekly payment' is a fixed amount you receive for the duration of the show's run and won't be subject to change.
- A 'minimum weekly royalty' is a guaranteed weekly payment. In this instance, if the show becomes very successful you may be entitled to more.

- In commercial theatre you may be allocated 'points in the royalty pool' which will pay you a portion of the profit if the show recoups.
- You may receive a 'percentage of net profit', although this is extremely rare.

Self-employment

Self-employment is not for everyone. It affords you a great amount of freedom, but at the expense of risk and a substantial lack of security. You will be in charge of your own scheduling and time-management and must always be on the lookout for new work. Composers in theatre are not afforded the luxury of 'selective creativity'. If you can't deliver on deadlines, your career will be pretty short-lived. You must be able to write music on spec, quickly and often under great amounts of pressure. You also need to be able to communicate with your director and creative team, and remain open and cooperative with the unique process attached to each individual production.

Despite being their own business, a successful theatre composer must remain engaged with the industry around them. They must retain a passion for theatre and a thirst for artistic invention, all whilst learning more about their trade and studying the art of composition.

Copyright

When you write music for a show, it is common practice for you as the composer to retain the copyright. A producer will commission you to write music and then effectively hire the right to use it for a specific period. If the production goes on to have another life after the original run has ended, the producer will have to renegotiate terms and pay you again to use your score.

Agents

An agent is not primarily there to get you work. You will find most of your own work through your relationships with directors and producers. However, an agent will negotiate contracts on your behalf, collect your fees, advise you on career options, introduce you to other industry professionals and generally support and champion you. I was desperate to get an agent when starting out in my career, but the reality is, an agent won't take you on unless you are in a position to prove you can get work and can make it worth their time. I had headlined my own concert at the Apollo Theatre and written successful musicals at the Edinburgh Festival Fringe, but it wasn't until I got a job at the Bush Theatre that agents really took an interest. This wasn't a bad thing. You have to work your own way into the industry because that's how you'll survive in it. Don't expect an agent to pick you up from nowhere and give you a career. It doesn't happen like that. You have to be travelling in a direction first, then an agent will be able to work with you and suggest some new paths to consider.

Meeting Directors

Directors see a lot of theatre and will constantly be looking to find new collaborators. If they like your work and think you might suit a project they have coming up, they may request to meet with you. Sometimes these are general meetings where a director just wants to know more about you and your work for potential future projects, and sometimes they request to meet you with a specific production in mind. In either case, make sure you go to the meeting prepared. Read up on a director – their background and their productions. Go to see one of their shows if possible, or at the very least read some reviews. If you're meeting up about a specific play, read it carefully and formulate some of your own general ideas about it, but you don't necessarily need to go the meeting with a pitch, as you've no idea how the director might want to tackle the production anyway.

The first thing they are most likely to ask you in direct reference to the play is simply what you thought or how it affected you personally. Be honest and forthcoming, but bear in mind that the director has chosen to direct it, so be open to its potential and don't shoot yourself in the foot at such an early stage by disparaging it. Ask them their thoughts on the play – where the idea to stage it came from or any previous productions they might have seen. You might find that a director has a completely unique relationship to a play and a reason for doing it that will unlock your ideas further. Working in theatre is all about relationships, so the director will be partly sussing out whether or not he thinks you will get on and work well together. If nothing else, it's always good to meet new people in the industry. Even if you don't end up working on this project together, once the connection is made it's more than likely you will run into each other again.

Societies

There are several industry bodies to which you may find it useful to belong.

- **The Musicians' Union (MU)** offers career and legal advice, protects your rights and insures you against 'public liability'. It has 'specialist full–time officials available to immediately tackle the issues raised by musicians working in the live arena, the recording studio, or when writing and composing. Such issues can range from copyright protection to valuable contractual advice, or from the recovery of unpaid fees to crucial work in health and safety.' (www.musiciansunion.org.uk)[71]
- **The British Academy of Songwriters, Composers and Authors (BASCA)** 'exists to support and protect the artistic, professional, commercial and copyright interests of songwriters, lyricists and composers of all genres of music and to celebrate and encourage excellence in British music writing'. (www.basca.org.uk)[72]

- **The Performing Rights Society (PRS)** and **Mechanical Copyright Protection Society (MCPS)** are now combined. They 'license organisations to play and perform music, and they make copyright music available on behalf of their members and those of overseas societies, distributing the royalties to them fairly and efficiently'. (www.prsformusic.com)[73]

Befriending Your Contemporaries

Composing music for theatre is a relatively unique profession. You don't tend to bump into other composers when working on productions, but as you build a career it's likely you will start to get to know your peers. I look forward to bumping into other composers at various industry events, having a drink and sharing experiences. Doing this with others who are tackling the same career path can be incredibly liberating and help to put all your concerns in context. Support one another and don't be afraid to ask each other's advice. It might seem natural to feel competitive, but in reality I have never found that to be at all useful. Everyone is doing their own thing, making their own way and building their own relationships. It's inevitable at times that a job will go someone else's way, but remember that people's careers blossom at different times and in different directions. If composers are artists, and if we can all agree that art is subjective, then we're unable to compete directly anyway. Over the span of a career, I would prefer to show my fellow artists support (and have them in my supportive camp too) rather than have us harbour unnecessary animosity towards each other. As Béla Bartók said: 'Competitions are for horses, not artists.'

Curtain Call

I've often comforted myself with the notion that in writing a book I would be forced to ask questions about why I do things the way I do, examine how music functions in plays, and think about why it might be worth doing in the first place. In a sense, I was intrigued to learn more about the profession and my relationship to it. After having set down my thoughts in ink, I've realised that I think it's the thirst for learning which is probably the biggest prerequisite a composer needs to have. Tackling a book about the process of composing for plays was one thing, but the real fascination still lies in the process of developing as an artist. Perhaps, in conclusion, the most useful anecdote and piece of advice I can impart is a story about one of the all-time greats...

In February 1827 whilst he lay on his deathbed, Beethoven, having received the scores of the complete works of Handel as a gift, told the young Gerhard von Breuning: 'Handel is the greatest and ablest of all composers; from him I can still learn. Bring me the books!'[74] The story goes that he would lie in bed and prop the scores up against the wall to study them. Even at the end of his life, Beethoven recognised the importance of learning and never wanted to stop.[75]

Who knows what the next score you'll write might teach you? Who knows what story you've yet to tell?

If composing music is an infinite resource (and it is), then your greatest score is still waiting to be written.

What could be more fascinating than that?

'Simplicity is the final achievement.
After one has played a vast quantity of notes
and more notes, it is simplicity that emerges
as the crowning reward of art.'

Frédéric Chopin

Acknowledgements

Mat Bartram, Daniel Bruce, Claire Bryan, Carolyn Downing, Peter Duchan, Terry Eldridge, Diana Glazer, Simon Godwin, Sunita Hinduja, Joe Hood, Chloe McGregor, Steven McIntosh, Laura Newman, Charlotte Padgham, Lindsay Posner, Hannah Price, Nick Quinn, Josie Rourke, Matthew Scott, Christopher Shutt, Lyndsey Turner, Cath Welsby, Kate West.

Endnotes

1. Richard Parncutt, 'Prenatal and infant conditioning, the mother schema, and the origins of music and religion' (2006)
2. http://www.britannica.com/art/incidental-music
3. Carol Kimball, 'In Sweet Music Is Such Art', *Journal of Singing* (2013)
4. *Henslowe's Diary*, ed. R.A. Foakes (2nd edition, 2002), pp. 317–18
5. http://www.vam.ac.uk/content/articles/0-9/18th-century-theatre/
6. http://www.bl.uk/romantics-and-victorians/articles/19th-century-theatre#
7. http://www.bl.uk/romantics-and-victorians/articles/19th-century-theatre#
8. http://www.britannica.com/art/incidental-music
9. http://www.nytimes.com/2010/07/20/arts/music/20incidental.html?_r=0
10. http://www.bbc.co.uk/programmes/p020cnxy
11. http://www.thebodysoulconnection.com/EducationCenter/fight.html
12. http://hyperphysics.phy-astr.gsu.edu/hbase/sound/infrasound.html
13. https://borderlandsciences.org/journal/vol/52/no4/Vassilatos_on_Vladimir_Gavreau.html
14. http://acp.eugraph.com/elephetc/infra.html
15. http://www.parascience.org.uk/articles/PScience%20Infrasound.pdf
16. http://www.amazon.co.uk/Lost-Science-Gerry-Vassilatos/dp/0932813755
17. Vic Tandy, 'The Ghost in the Machine', *Journal of the Society for Psychical Research* 62 (1998)
18. http://news.bbc.co.uk/1/hi/sci/tech/3087674.stm
19. *Ibid.*

20. https://www.prsformusic.com/SiteCollectionDocuments/PPS%20Tariffs/T-2014-01%20Tariff.pdf
21. *Moulin Rouge* (dir. Baz Lurhmann, 2001)
22. https://www.prsformusic.com/SiteCollectionDocuments/PPS%20Leaflets/MusicinTheatres.pdf
23. https://www.wordnik.com/words/melodrama
24. http://www.theguardian.com/music/2005/aug/19/classicalmusicandopera.edinburghfestival2005
25. Amanda Mabillard, 'Shakespeare's Audience: The Groundlings' (Shakespeare Online, 20 August 2000), accessed 27 July 2015
26. https://soundcloud.com/nationaltheatre/simon-godwin-on-strange
27. http://www.merriam-webster.com/dictionary/parody
28. Mikhail Bakhtin, *Creation of a Prosaics*: http://www.sup.org/books/title/?id=2937
29. http://www.merriam-webster.com/dictionary/pastiche
30. Fredric Jameson, *The Cultural Turn: Selected Writings on the Post-modern, 1983–1998* (1998), p. 4
31. https://fashion-trends.knoji.com/postmodern-parody-and-pastiche/
32. Richard Middleton, *Key Terms in Popular Music and Culture* (1999): 'Form' (p. 141)
33. *Ibid.*
34. Catherine Schmidt-Jones, *The Basic Elements of Music* (2013): 'Form in Music'
35. Middleton, *Key Terms*, p. 142
36. *Ibid.*
37. *Ibid.*
38. Wallace Berry, *Form in Music* (2nd edition, 1985), p. 4.
39. *The Tempest*, ed. David Lindley (New Cambridge Shakespeare, 2002), p. 251
40. H.B. Lathrop, 'Shakespeare's Dramatic Use of Songs', *Modern Language Notes* 23 (1908); Shakespeare Online (20 August 2013)
41. http://www.virginiacitymusic.com/instruments.html
42. Lathrop, 'Shakespeare's Dramatic Use of Songs'
43. Stephen Sondheim, *Finishing the Hat: Collected Lyrics 1954–1981* (2010), p. xviii
44. *Ibid.*
45. http://www.soundonsound.com/sos/jan01/articles/lyric.asp
46. *Ibid.*

47. *Ibid.*
48. *Ibid.*
49. *Ibid.*
50. Sondheim, *Finishing the Hat*, p. xxvi
51. http://www.jiscdigitalmedia.ac.uk/guide/acoustic-treatment
52. http://www.musiciansunion.org.uk/Home/Advice/Playing-Live/Working-in-Theatre
53. http://www.musiciansunion.org.uk/Files/Rates/Recording-Rates/BPI-MU-Agreement
54. *Ibid.*
55. http://www.musiciansunion.org.uk/wp-content/uploads/2012/02/ABO-MU-Agreement-2013-2014.pdf
56. http://www.musiciansunion.org.uk/Files/Rates/Recording-Rates/BPI-MU-Agreement
57. http://www.musiciansunion.org.uk/getattachment/1d69781d-f339-4784-af8f-2dbc258ed0d0/RNT-MU-rates.aspx
58. SOLT MU Agreement October 2014
59. http://www.theguardian.com/stage/2008/jan/24/theatre.musicals
60. *Ibid.*
61. *Ibid.*
62. http://www.associationofsounddesigners.com/whatis
63. http://www.prsformusic.com/users/businessesandliveevents/Pages/DoIneedalicence.aspx
64. https://www.prsformusic.com/SiteCollectionDocuments/PPS%20Leaflets/MusicinTheatres.pdf
65. *Ibid.*
66. *Ibid.*
67. *The Imagineering Workout*, ed. Peggy Van Pelt
68. http://www.nesta.org.uk/news/research-finds-national-theatre-live-has-no-negative-impact-regional-theatre-going
69. http://www.indielondon.co.uk/Theatre-Review/donmar-and-channel-4-announce-record-viewing-figures-for-the-vote
70. http://www.channel4.com/info/press/news/viewing-success-for-channel-4s-alternative-election-coverage
71. www.musiciansunion.org.uk
72. basca.org.uk
73. www.prsformusic.com
74. http://www.gutenberg.org/files/3528/3528-h/3528-h.htm#link2H_4_0009
75. http://www.musesmuse.com/ea-greatmusician.html

facebook.com/nickhernbooks
twitter.com/nickhernbooks